Antonia Ballare & Angelique Lampros

BEHAVIOR SMART!

Ready-to-Use Activities
for Building
Personal and Social Skills
for Grades K-4

Illustrations by Eileen Gerne Ciavarella & Carrie Oesmann

THE CENTER FOR APPLIED
RESEARCH IN EDUCATION
West Nyack, New York 10995

10 9 8 7 6 5 4 3 2 1

Library of Congress Cataloging-in-Publication Data

Ballare, Antonia.
   Behavior smart! : ready-to-use activities for building personal
and social skills in grades K-4 / Antonia Ballare & Angelique
Lampros ; illustrations by Eileen Gerne Ciavarella & Carrie Desmann.
       p.   cm.
   ISBN 0-87628-172-2
 1. Social skills—Study and teaching (Elementary)—United States.
 2. Social skills—United States—Problems, exercises, etc.
 I. Lampros, Angelique.   II. Title.
 HQ783.B29   1994
 372.83—dc20   93-42750
                                                     CIP

ISBN 0-87628-172-2

Original Music © 1994 by Robert Winder, Jr.

**The Center for Applied
Research in Education**
Business Information & Publishing Division
West Nyack, NY 10995
Simon & Schuster, A Paramount Communications Company

Printed in the United States of America

To our families for their love and support
and
To our fathers, who would have been proud

ABOUT THE AUTHORS

Antonia Ballare earned her B.S. from Trenton State College in New Jersey and her M.Ed. in Elementary Reading from Boston University. She has been an elementary teacher for over 25 years and is currently teaching fourth grade.

Angelique Lampros earned her B.A. from Montclair State College in New Jersey and her M.A. in Elementary Administration from George Washington University. Having more than 30 years' experience, she is currently a basic skills/resource teacher. She has taught at both the elementary and secondary levels and has been an acting principal.

The authors are colleagues at Seth Boyden School in Maplewood, New Jersey, and close friends. They first met while teaching at Jefferson School in the district of South Orange-Maplewood, New Jersey. Similar philosophies of education led them to collaborate in team-teaching, the development of management techniques, and the writing of *The Classroom Organizer: 201 Ready-to-Use Forms for K-8 Teachers and Administrators,* also published by The Center for Applied Research in Education.

ABOUT THIS BOOK

Behavior Smart! Ready-to-Use Activities for Building Personal and Social Skills in Grades K-4 provides high-interest, easy-to-use activities and step-by-step techniques for developing positive group behavior in children. Included are 65 multi-page reproducible student activity sheets and teacher-directed activities that guide children in their interactions with peers and adults in the classroom setting, the school, and the community.

All activities in this book are *child-centered*, providing humorous, real-life problem situations—illustrated with lively animal characters—that invite children to work out their own solutions. Children are encouraged to identify behaviors of their own that need improvement, laugh at themselves, solve problems and, eventually, apply strategies for interacting positively with other people.

Behavior Smart! is divided into eight sections of activities for developing over 40 specific social skills as described in the Contents/Skills Index at the beginning of the book. A different animal character acts as a guide for good behavior for each grade level: Kanga Kangaroo for kindergarten, Randy Raccoon for grade 1, Perry Penguin for grade 2, Chee Chee Chimp for grade 3, and Ginger Giraffe for grade 4. As a handy reference, grade levels are also indicated on the Contents/Skills Index.

Here is a brief description of what you will find in each section:

- Section I, "Are You Great in a Group?" shows students how to become responsible and contributing members of different groups. Highlighted skills include patience, cooperation, assertiveness, and good sportsmanship.
- Section II, "Do You Value Diversity?" heightens students' appreciation for the contributions and diversity of all people.
- Section III, "Are You a Friendly Friend?" focuses on acquiring and keeping friends, and becoming trustworthy and caring.
- Section IV, "Are You a Tactful Talker?" guides students in becoming tactful talkers. Activities encourage respectful, supportive, and politely assertive language.
- Section V, "Would You Applaud Your Audience Behavior?" makes students aware of appropriate behaviors as audience members.
- Section VI, "Would You Win Votes for Visiting?" prepoares students for visiting someone's home and taking family or field trips by identifying good manners and behavior. Included is a game called "Destination U.S.A."
- Section VII, "Do Your Table Manners Make It?" teaches students progressively demanding table manners required in different situations. Included is a game called "Posh Nosh."
- Section VIII, "Are Your Looks Likeable?" shows students how to convey a likeable appearance by means of good personaly hygiene, positive facial expression and body language, and suitable clothing choices.

The Appendix at the end of *Behavior Smart!* offers you a glossary of terms commonly used with behavior. You'll also find additional information and materials that will help you work with parents and students in developing the children's personal and social skills.

It is never too early to teach children appropriate behaviors for being members of a family, a class, a school community, and society as a whole. Children must learn to interact with other children and adults on a daily basis in a variety of settings. *Behavior Smart! Ready-to-Use Activities for Building Personal and Social Skills in Grades K-4* will help children do just that!

Antonia Ballare
Angelique Lampros

CONTENTS/SKILLS INDEX

Section I: Are You Great in a Group? • 1

Section I

ARE YOU GREAT IN A GROUP?

Section I focuses on behaviors relevant to three or more persons and helps students learn to make decisions that are respectful of others' rights. These activities emphasize the desirable qualities necessary for positive group interaction.

Activity / Grade Level / Description

I-1 *Making Wise Choices* (**K–4**) is a set of twenty discussion activities for each school day of the month. The students are invited to determine appropriate reactions and responses to hypothetical group situations of the kinds presented throughout Section I.

I-2 *Want My Glue?* (**K**) requires you to focus the students' attention on ways of sharing and working together in the classroom. Suggested questions are: What do you see in the picture that shows boys and girls sharing? What must we share in our own classroom? How can we work better together? What does the title of the activity really mean?

When given too few materials—such as scissors, crayons, markers, etc., in each group—students will have to share as each completes the empty face on sheet I-2B as his or her own. Those students who shared particularly well can be rewarded by seeing their faces on a bulletin board or by wearing them around their necks.

1-3 *It's Not Whether You Win or Lose, It's How You Play the Game* (**K-1**) reinforces, by means of three illustrations, the expectation that children will follow the rules when playing Musical Chairs, Hide-and-Seek, Candyland®, and other group games. At the end of the lesson, with input from students, you establish reasonable consequences and rewards. For example: **consequence**—timeout from the game; **reward**—"Good Sport Game Chart" on which stars are placed after the names of "good sports" in the class.

I-4 *Shh! Shh! Shh!* (**K-2**) is a rhyming activity that teaches proper behavior in the library. (**Answers:** slow, fine, quiet, reaching, look, help, out, return)

1

I-5   *Were You Here First?* (K-4) is a wanted poster that demonstrates polite behavior while waiting in line (at the sink, drinking fountain or bathroom), waiting around a table for materials, and waiting for a conversation to end so as not to interrupt. Pose students accordingly, then photograph them or have them choose a scene to draw in the space provided on the activity sheet. Write a desired attribute after the word WANTED. This activity may be easily adapted to any section of this book by using white correction fluid on the title of the activity sheet.

I-6   *Leader or Follower?* (2-4) presents students with the responsibilities of being leaders and group members and invites them to assume one of these roles while completing mobiles related to the subject.

I-7   *Best Behavior* (K-4) is a matching activity that reinforces thoughtful, polite and sensitive group behavior. It can be expanded into a bulletin board or Big Book if desired.

I-8   *Am I a Tattletale?* (K-4) provides ten scenes to stimulate discussion that will teach students the difference between being a tattletale and seeking help when the situation warrants it. Although sheet I-8A is suggested for kindergarten, I-8B for grade 1, I-8C for grade 2, I-8D for grade 3, and I-8E for grade 4, you may find more than one of them helpful. Discussion should lead students to understand that if health/safety or personal/public property is violated, the help of someone in authority should be sought.

       The children are to decide what situation is illustrated by each drawing; determine their comparative severity, that is, what the possible consequences are for the victim and for the aggressor; and decide what could happen as a result of "telling" or "not telling."

       The last page of the activity directs students to draw personal experiences that are related to the concept and, thereby, evaluates their understanding. This could be followed by role-playing where students might apply the concepts.

I-9   *Yes, Sir!* (K-4) teaches respectful acknowledgment of authority—experience, knowledge, and title—to students.

I-10   *Please Stand* (K-4) encourages respect for tradition.

I-11   *Sticks and Stones* (1-2) encourages children to speak kindly to others. To reinforce this concept, stickers or other rewards may be given.

I-12   *Are You Being Bossy?* (1-2) creates an awareness, with three illustrations, of the effect that being bossy has on others and the consequences for the bossy person.

I-13   *It's Not My Job!* (1-4) uses two record sheets to foster a sense of responsibility in sharing tasks within the group in the classroom, in the school, and at home.

I-14   *Hurry! Hurry!* (2-3) is a simple board game that focuses attention on the positive aspects of being prompt and the negative consequences of being late. This makes an effective enrichment activity.

I-15 *I Didn't Get Invited!* (2-3) is a cartoon that invites discussion to promote awareness of the ways that thoughtless comments can make someone feel excluded. It leads to the development of a thoughtful attitude towards the feelings of others in social situations.

I-16 *What Do I Do Now?* (2-4) helps to develop patience and provides suggested activities for using "free" time profitably in school.

I-17 *Better We Than Me* (2-4) promotes appreciation for what a group can accomplish that an individual cannot. Divide the class into two hetero-geneous groups of equal size. One group consists of individuals working alone for ten minutes to list rules of polite behavior. Subdivide the second group into smaller groups. Give the groups ten minutes to brainstorm with a competent writer acting as recorder. Tally the final results for the individuals versus the groups. There should be many more rules listed by the groups. Elicit from the class other situations in which members of a group, by supporting each other, can produce more than an individual can (family, play production, chorus, club, orchestra, team, etc.).

I-18 *It's Family Meeting Time* (3-4) is an activity sheet that fosters cooperation among members of a group of related people, such as a class, household, or other small group. It focuses attention on the process of identifying a problem, discussing it, and arriving at a solution. It is best used first during a class meeting to solve a classroom problem. A copy of the same form may then be sent home for members of households to conduct their own meeting. Written parental or oral student response is invited.

I-19 *I'll Get You!* (3-4) is a role-playing activity. The tactics provided help students avoid being physically and verbally abusive in confrontational situations.

I-20 *Should I or Shouldn't I?* (3-4) is a modified version of both Tic-Tac-Toe and Bingo to help students recognize the negative influence of a group in order to decide not to participate. Students have to determine whether or not the subsequent action on the game sheet is the appropriate one and why. A discussion of answers and their reasons—whether before, during or after the game—can help the individual make the right decision as it pertains to group influence.

I-21 *Dodging More Than the Ball!* (3) is a cartoon illustrating the verbal insensitivity many children have experienced while playing a competitive game. After reading and discussing the comments of the chimps on the first page, develop a list of rules for good sportsmanship on the second page. The third page can be used individually or with the whole class (as a transpar-ency) to write sensitive comments that reflect good sportsmanship.

I-22 *It's Your Bathroom!* (4) deals with vandalism, the mischievous or malicious destruction or damage of property. Be sure that students understand the difference between vandalism and accidental loss or harm before directing small groups to examine the drawings in order to brainstorm possible solu-tions. Then list them during whole class discussion.

I-1   *MAKING WISE CHOICES*

Day 1   A friend asks for the marker you want to use. You . . .

Day 2   A classmate wants to take out the same book you want. You . . .

Day 3   You enter the classroom during the flag salute. You . . .

Day 4   You enter the auditorium after the program has begun. You . . .

Day 5   Someone grabs the ball from you in the gym. You . . .

Day 6   You don't like the snack that is being passed out. You . . .

Day 7   Someone falls off his chair. You . . .

Day 8   No one wants to be the notetaker in your small group. You . . .

Day 9   You can't find the money you had in your desk. You . . .

Day 10   You want to ask your teacher a question, but she is speaking with someone else. You . . .

Day 11   You have finished all your classwork. You . . .

Day 12   When playing dodgeball, someone calls you a nasty name. You . . .

Day 13   A classmate whispers to you during a spelling test. You . . .

Day 14   There is a substitute teacher for the day. You . . .

Day 15   You're planning a party and want to hand out invitations. You . . .

Day 16   A classmate is tapping a pencil on the desk while you are reading. It is annoying you. You . . .

Day 17   The principal walks into the room. You . . .

Day 18   Someone steps on your foot while walking past your desk. You . . .

Day 19   While in the bathroom you see a group marking the walls. You . . .

Day 20   There's a little glue left in the bottle. Both you and a classmate need some. You . . .

I-2A   WANT MY GLUE?

Section I: Are You Great in a Group?

I-2B   WANT MY GLUE?

TODAY
I SHARED.

Section I: Are You Great in a Group?

I-3   IT'S NOT WHETHER YOU WIN OR LOSE, IT'S HOW YOU PLAY THE GAME

I-4   SHH! SHH! SHH!

In line to the library I will go,
Not too fast and not too _ _ _ _ .

I will return my books on time,
So I won't have to pay a _ _ _ _ .

When I get there I won't riot,
I'll sit down and be real _ _ _ _ _ .

While listening to the librarian teaching,
I will not for a book be _ _ _ _ _ _ _ _ .

When it's time to get a book,
I'll quietly get up and _ _ _ _ .

If a book is not there, I shall not yelp;
But, simply go and ask for _ _ _ _ .

I'll select another and not pout,
Then go have the book checked _ _ _ .

While turning pages I will learn,
Until to our classroom we'll _ _ _ _ _ _ .

Name _____ Date _____

I-5   *WERE YOU HERE FIRST?*

WANTED: _____

I-6A   LEADER OR FOLLOWER?

DIRECTIONS:

1. Determine the make-up of the group: number and members.

2. Either select or elect a leader.

3. The leader reads aloud, one at a time, all 24 roles listed on pages I-6F through I-6I for a vote by the group.

4. At the top of each box is a small circle. The leader prints "F" for "Follower" or "L" for "Leader" as the group decides whose role it describes. If the group cannot reach a consensus, the leader puts a "?" in the circle for reconsideration later by process of elimination. There are twelve boxes for each of the two roles.

5. After every box has been labeled, the leader takes the answers to the teacher for a final check.

6. Each group is ready to make either a LEADER mobile or a FOLLOWER mobile or both. (See sheet I-6B.) The class will decide on a color (marker, crayon and/or construction paper) to distinguish LEADER mobiles from FOLLOWER mobiles.

I-6B   LEADER OR FOLLOWER?

Materials Needed:

- Sheets I-6F through I-6I

- Scissors

- String

- Something sturdy to attach strings; i.e., wire hangers, cardboard, dowel

- Hole puncher or stapler

- Marker, crayon, or construction paper

- Optional: reinforcements, glue

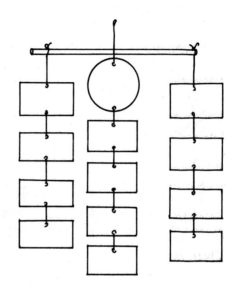

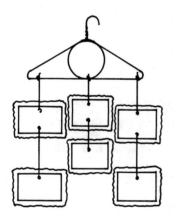

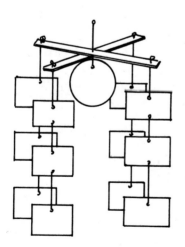

Group Tasks:

1. Cut boxes.

2. Decide on design of mobile.

3. Cut string to fit design selected.

4. Color boxes or use construction paper backing.

5. Attach strings to boxes and title.

6. Complete balanced mobile and hang.

I-6C   LEADER OR FOLLOWER?

BEING A FOLLOWER

I-6D   LEADER OR FOLLOWER?

BEING
A
LEADER

Name _____ Date _____

I-6E   *LEADER OR FOLLOWER?*

	NAME	TASK
LEADER:	_____	_____
FOLLOWER:	_____	_____
FOLLOWER:	_____	_____
FOLLOWER:	_____	_____
FOLLOWER:	_____	_____
FOLLOWER:	_____	_____
FOLLOWER:	_____	_____

- -

Name _____ Date _____

LEADER OR FOLLOWER?

HOW DID I DO?

Write Y for yes, N for no, or S for sometimes:

1. I listened.   _____
2. I contributed.   _____
3. I shared.   _____
4. I cooperated.   _____
5. I had fun.   _____

Please show your answers to everyone who worked in your group.
Do they agree with your view of yourself?

_____

_____

_____

Section I: Are You Great in a Group?

Name _____ Date _____

I-6F   LEADER OR FOLLOWER?

◯	◯
Understand the task and explain it to the group.	Be ready to accept the role of leader at another time.
◯	◯
Wait your turn.	Ask for a vote when there is disagreement.
◯	◯
Be ready to accept the role of follower at another time.	Allow the leader to lead.

Section I: Are You Great in a Group?

I-6G   LEADER OR FOLLOWER?

◯

Call upon members of the group equally.

◯

Invite group members to do what they are good at.

◯

Stay on the task.

◯

Let the leader know when the group has a problem it can't solve.

◯

Volunteer to do what you are good at.

◯

Offer good suggestions.

I-6H   LEADER OR FOLLOWER?

◯

React politely to all ideas
whether or not you
agree.

◯

Ask for the teacher's help
when the group has a
problem it can't solve.

◯

Accept the decision of
the group after a vote.

◯

Keep the group on task.

◯

Encourage respect among
group members by being
polite.

◯

Cheerfully accept the
task you are given.

I-6I   LEADER OR FOLLOWER?

○

Pay attention to the person speaking without interrupting.

○

Give the completed work (project, report, solution, etc.) to the teacher.

○

Recognize the talents of group members.

○

Offer good suggestions.

○

Help each other.

○

Direct the group step-by-step through the task.

I-6J   LEADER OR FOLLOWER?

ANSWER SHEET:

LEADER	FOLLOWER
1. Understand the task and explain it to the group.	1. Offer good suggestions.
2. Call upon members of the group equally.	2. Wait your turn.
3. Keep the group on task.	3. Pay attention to the person who is speaking without interrupting.
4. Encourage respect among group members by being polite.	4. React politely to all ideas whether or not you agree.
5. Offer good suggestions.	5. Stay on the task.
6. Ask for a vote when there is a disagreement.	6. Accept the decision of the group after a vote.
7. Ask for the teacher's help when the group has a problem it can't solve.	7. Let the leader know when the group has a problem it can't solve.
8. Recognize the talents of group members.	8. Volunteer to do what you are good at.
9. Invite group members to do what they are good at.	9. Cheerfully accept the task you are given.
10. Direct the group step-by-step through the task.	10. Help each other.
11. Give the completed work (project, report, solution, etc.) to the teacher.	11. Allow the leader to lead.
12. Be ready to accept the role of follower at another time.	12. Be ready to accept the role of leader at another time.

I-7A   BEST BEHAVIOR

1. TAKE THE ANIMAL SHEET OR SHEETS GIVEN TO YOU.

2. CUT OUT THE ILLUSTRATIONS AND KEEP THEM TOGETHER.

3. CUT OUT THE SENTENCES AND KEEP THEM TOGETHER.

4. DECIDE WHICH ILLUSTRATION BELONGS WITH EACH SENTENCE.

5. PASTE THE ILLUSTRATION IN THE "TUMMY" OF YOUR ANIMAL AND THE MATCHING SENTENCE AT THE BOTTOM OF THE PAGE.

Section I: Are You Great in a Group?

Name _____ Date _____

I-7B   BEST BEHAVIOR

Share things.	Close your mouth while chewing.
Wash your hands.	Walk up and down the stairs.
Say, "Please."	Say, "Thank you."
Say, "Excuse me."	Say, "I'm sorry."
Have your name on your belongings.	Be kind.

I-7C   BEST BEHAVIOR

Keep hands and feet to yourself.	Take care of property.
Be safe.	Be helpful.
Read silently.	Say, "May I?"
Say, "Hello."	Say, "Goodbye."
Keep your space neat.	Say, "You're welcome."

I-7D   BEST BEHAVIOR

Cover your mouth.	Throw scraps away.
Keep feet on the floor.	Laugh at yourself.
Raise your hand.	Listen.
Walk in the hallway.	Share space.
Wait your turn.	Walk in back of a speaker.

I-7E   BEST BEHAVIOR

Section I: Are You Great in a Group?

I-7F BEST BEHAVIOR

I-7G   BEST BEHAVIOR

Section I: Are You Great in a Group?

I-7H   BEST BEHAVIOR

Section I: Are You Great in a Group?

I-71   BEST BEHAVIOR

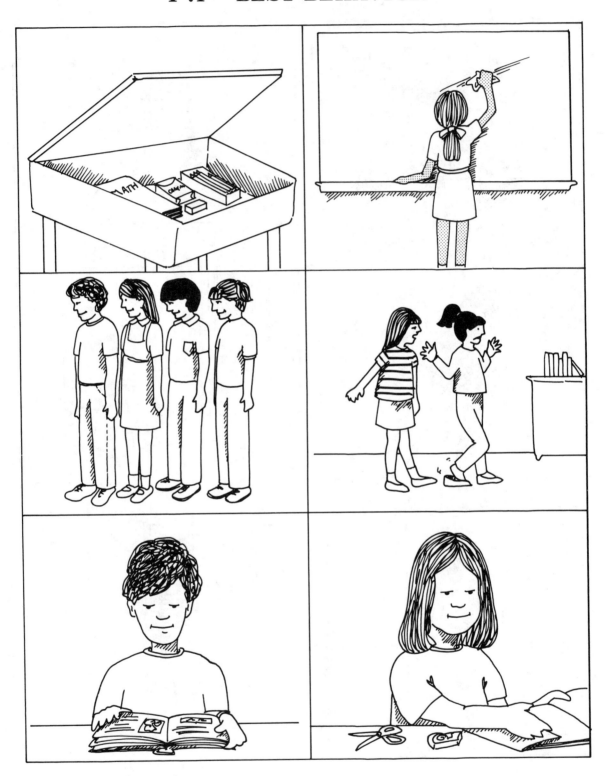

Section I: Are You Great in a Group?

I-7J   BEST BEHAVIOR

Section I: Are You Great in a Group?

I-7K   BEST BEHAVIOR

Section I: Are You Great in a Group?

I-7L   *BEST BEHAVIOR*

Section I: Are You Great in a Group?

I-7M   BEST BEHAVIOR

Section I: Are You Great in a Group?

I-7N   BEST BEHAVIOR

Section I: Are You Great in a Group?

I-8A   AM I A TATTLETALE?

I-8B   AM I A TATTLETALE?

I-8C   AM I A TATTLETALE?

I-8D AM I A TATTLETALE?

I-8E   AM I A TATTLETALE?

Name _____ Date _____

I-8F   AM I A TATTLETALE?

Draw your own picture to show an action happening that <u>you need to tell</u> and an action happening where <u>you would be a tattletale.</u>

<u>You</u> <u>NEED</u> <u>TO</u> <u>TELL</u>!

<u>DON'T BE A TATTLETALE!</u>

I-9   YES SIR!

I-10   PLEASE STAND

Name ——————— Date ———————

I-11 STICKS AND STONES

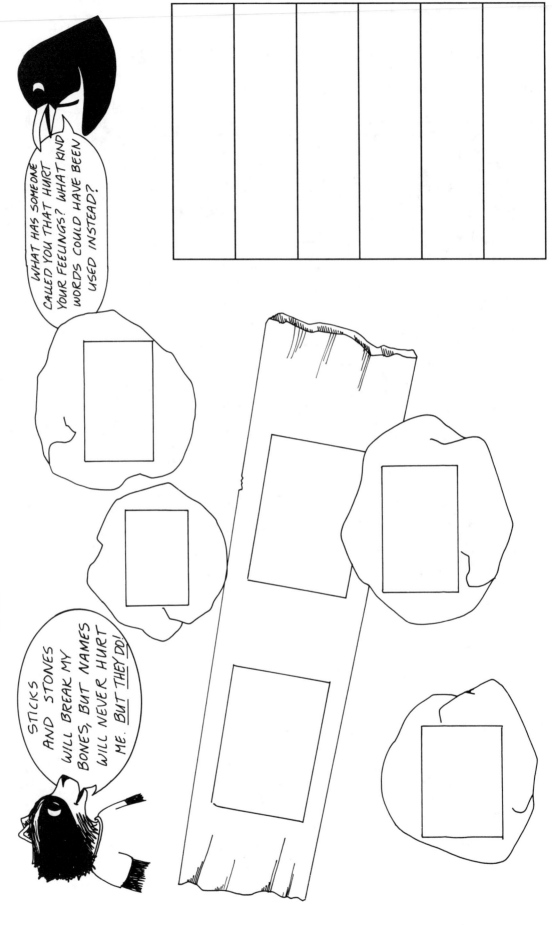

I-12   ARE YOU BEING BOSSY?

Name _____ Date _____

I-13A   IT'S NOT MY JOB!

BUT IT IS! PUT YES OR NO IN EACH BOX. HAVE YOUR PARENT WRITE A COMMENT ON THE OTHER SIDE OF THIS SHEET.

AT HOME:

Responsibility	Monday	Tuesday	Wednesday	Thursday	Friday
Organization—Did I . . .					
1. Make My Bed?					
2. Keep My Room Neat?					
3. Get Notices Signed?					
4. Put All School Materials in One Place?					
5. Hang Up My Clothes?					
6. Put My Dirty Clothes in the Hamper?					
7. Select My Clothes for the Next Day?					
8.					

Section I: Are You Great in a Group?

I-13A IT'S NOT MY JOB! (continued)

Responsibility	Monday	Tuesday	Wednesday	Thursday	Friday
Chores—Did I . . .					
1. Take Care of My Pet(s)?					
2. Set and/or Clear the Table?					
3. Help Prepare the Meal?					
4.					
5.					
Grooming—Did I . . .					
1. Wash My Hands (After Bathroom Use, After School and Before Meals)?					
2. Wash My Face?					
3. Brush My Teeth?					
4. Take a Bath or Shower?					
5. Wash My Hair?					
6.					
Work and Play—Did I . . .					
1. Do My Homework?					
2. Practice My Musical Instrument?					
3.					

Section I: Are You Great in a Group?

Name _____

Date _____

I-13B   IT'S NOT MY JOB!

BUT IT IS! PUT Y FOR YES, S FOR SOMETIMES, N FOR NO IN EACH BOX. GIVE THIS SHEET TO YOUR TEACHER FOR A COMMENT AT THE END OF THE WEEK.

AT SCHOOL:

Responsibility	Monday	Tuesday	Wednesday	Thursday	Friday
In Class:					
1. Was I on time?					
2. Was I prepared?					
a. Outerwear					
b. Lunch					
c. Homework					
d. Signed notes/notices					
e.					
f.					
3. Did I do my class job?					
4. Did I follow the rules?					

Section I: Are You Great in a Group?

I-13B   IT'S NOT MY JOB! (continued)

Responsibility	Monday	Tuesday	Wednesday	Thursday	Friday
5. Did I work well?					
6. Did I organize my things for leaving?					
In School:					
1. Did I follow the rules?					
2. Did I clean up at lunch?					
3. Did I behave well?					
4. Did I walk quietly in the halls?					
5.					
6.					

Teacher's Comments: _____

_____

_____

Teacher's Initials _____

Section I: Are You Great in a Group?

I-13C   IT'S NOT MY JOB!

Section I: Are You Great in a Group?

I-14   HURRY! HURRY!

PLAYER #2

START / FINISH

YOU'RE ON TIME FOR LUNCH

YOU REALLY ENJOY TO YOUR FOOD.

LATE TO LUNCH.

GOBBLE FOOD AND GET INDIGESTION. YOU'RE...

YOU'RE ON TIME FOR SOCCER PRACTICE.

YOU WARM-UP AND CAN PLAY BETTER.

EVERYTIME YOU LAND ON A _LATE_ YOU GO BACK TO START/FINISH. THE FIRST PLAYER TO REACH THE OPPOSITE SIDE WINS. THE EXACT NUMBER OF MOVES IS NEEDED TO GET TO FINISH.

YOU'RE ON TIME FOR CLASS.

LATE TO BASEBALL PRACTICE.

YOU TALK TO YOUR FRIENDS AND GET READY FOR THE DAY.

YOU'RE ON TIME FOR DETENTION.

CAN'T PLAY.

PLAYER #4

START / FINISH

YOU AVOID GETTING INTO MORE TROUBLE.

FREE SPOT

LATE TO DENTIST.

MISS APPOINTMENT

LATE TO SCHOOL AUDITORIUM

THE PERFORMERS ARE ANNOYED.

YOU'RE RELAXED.

YOU GET TO THE THEATER ON TIME.

LATE TO CLASS

PLAYER #1

START / FINISH

MISSED DIRECTIONS

DIRECTIONS:
USE SPINNER OR DIE TO DETERMINE ORDER OF PLAYERS. HIGHEST NUMBER PLAYS FIRST. CAN BE PLAYED WITH 2-4 PLAYERS. USE SPINNER OR DIE TO DETERMINE MOVES.

LATE TO DETENTION.

LATE TO CONCERT. TIME IS DOUBLED.

WAIT UNTIL INTERMISSION BEFORE ENTERING.

YOU'RE ON TIME FOR THE DENTIST.

YOU GET IT OVER WITH

LATE TO CLASS: GO TO OFFICE.

PLAYER #3

START / FINISH

I-15   I DIDN'T GET INVITED!

Section I: Are You Great in a Group?

Name _____

Date _____

I-16A WHAT DO I DO NOW?

Week of _____

Monday
Tuesday
Wednesday
Thursday
Friday

3. WRITE THE ACTIVITY(IES) IN THE SPACE PROVIDED FOR EACH DAY OF THE WEEK.

1. LOOK AT THE LIST OF ACTIVITIES ON THE FOLLOWING PAGE.

2. DECIDE EACH MORNING ON ACTIVITY(IES) YOU CAN DO WHEN YOUR REGULAR CLASSROOM ASSIGNMENTS ARE COMPLETE.

Section I: Are You Great in a Group?

I-16B   *WHAT DO I DO NOW?*

List of Activities:

____ Write a story.
____ Make a Big Book.
____ Write in your journal.
____ Begin a diary.
____ Draw a picture.
____ Make your own pictionary.
____ Make your own dictionary.
____ Complete unfinished work.
____ Solve a math problem.

____ Read a book.
____ Clean your desk.
____ Go to the computer.
____ Make a diorama.
____ Make a mobile.
____ Do challenge-spelling.
____ Make up your own puzzle.
____ Go to a learning center.
____ Make a collage.

....

Learning Center Materials:

Math/Science

—flash cards
—math games and puzzles
—Cuisinaire® rods, powers-of-ten blocks
   or other manipulatives
—measurement devices
—materials for experiments
—record keeping and other activity sheets

Language/Social Studies

—blank cards and lined paper for writing
—dictionaries, thesauruses, encyclopedias,
   atlases, almanacs
—construction paper and oaktag
—scissors, staples, hole punch, tape, glue,
   string
—old magazines, current newspapers, shoeboxes
—letter stencils, activity sheets

Section I: Are You Great in a Group?

I-17   BETTER WE THAN ME!

THINK OF AS MANY RULES AS YOU CAN FOR POLITE BEHAVIOR.

YOU HAVE TEN MINUTES TO WRITE AS MANY AS POSSIBLE.

EXAMPLES: Wait your turn.

Cover your mouth.

_____

_____

_____

_____

_____

_____

_____

_____

_____

_____

_____

_____

_____

NUMBER EACH RULE AND USE AS MANY OF THESE SHEETS AS YOU NEED.

I-18   IT'S FAMILY MEETING TIME

MEMBERS: (for example, class/teacher; small group; household)

DATE: **TIME:**

AGENDA

I. PROBLEM(S):

II. DISCUSSION:

III. SOLUTION(S):

You are invited to communicate the results of your meeting to your teacher.

Section I: Are You Great in a Group?

I-19A   I'LL GET YOU!

Scene A

The class is told to quietly get on line for gym. Gerry is standing in back of his/her friend when Kanga cuts in front of Perry. Gerry steps out of line and smacks Kanga for getting in front of his/her friend.

Scene B

Randy can't find his/her book bag when it is time to go home. He/she starts to throw things around the coatroom, uses foul language, and kicks the lunch boxes around.

I-19B   I'LL GET YOU!

Scene C

Chee Chee receives a grade of 60% on his/her corrected math test and sees that Randy has 85% and Gerry 90% right. Chee Chee grabs and breaks Randy's pencil in half and throws it across the room.

Scene D

Kanga and Perry begin comparing the new sneakers they both have. Soon they are arguing about whose sneakers are better. Kanga has a longer list of reasons than Perry. Perry calls Kanga an insulting name.

Scene E

Kanga, Randy, Perry, Chee Chee, and Gerry are planning a class party. Each time Kanga, Randy, Perry, and Chee Chee offer a good idea, Gerry disagrees and insists that his/her ideas are better. They all start to fight instead of planning the party.

I-19C   I'LL GET YOU!

Scene A Questions

1. What happened here?
2. What else could Gerry have done?
3. Is it Gerry's job to be the judge and punisher of someone else's mistakes?

Scene B Questions

1. What happened here?
2. Did losing control solve the problem of the missing book bag?
3. What positive actions can Randy take when things happen unexpectedly?

Scene C Questions

1. What happened here?
2. Was Chee Chee jealous of Randy and Gerry?
3. How can Chee Chee deal with his/her jealousy next time?

Scene D Questions

1. What happened here?
2. How did Kanga's remarks make Perry feel?
3. How could Perry and Kanga have avoided making this a win-lose situation? How did they both lose?

Scene E Questions

1. What happened here?
2. Did Gerry's bossiness get the job done?
3. Did Kanga, Randy, Perry, and Chee Chee like working with someone who was bossy?

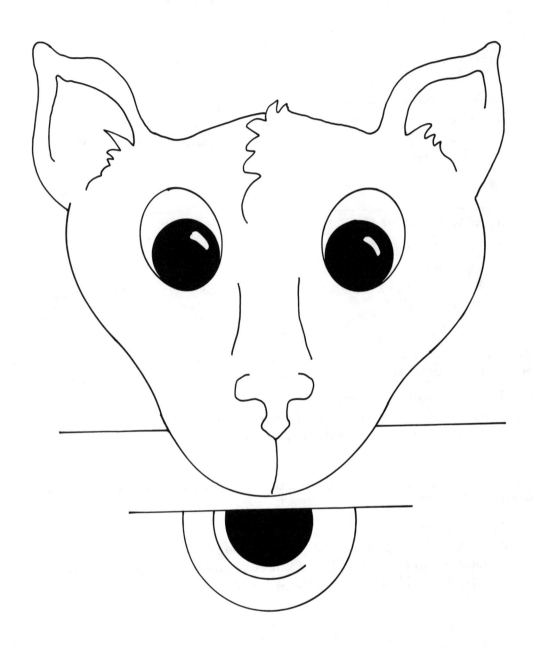

Section I: Are You Great in a Group?

Section I: Are You Great in a Group?

Section I: Are You Great in a Group?

Section I: Are You Great in a Group?

I-191 I'LL GET YOU!

THINK ABOUT THE WAYS LISTED BELOW TO HELP YOU KEEP YOUR COOL AND GET ALONG BETTER WITH EVERYONE. TRY USING ONE OF THESE TACTICS THE NEXT TIME YOU FIND YOURSELF GETTING ANGRY, WHATEVER THE REASON.

ASK YOURSELF:

1. Is this really worth my getting upset?

2. Imagine how you look and sound to others.

3. Ask the other person to explain what he or she really feels or means.

4. Make a list of your good qualities, talents, what you have that makes you special and lucky. If you really think about it, there are many.

5. Recognize the signs that you are about to explode with anger. Keep calm by thinking about something pleasant or begin counting something.

6. Recognize the signs when others are about to explode with anger. Back away or try to discuss calmly.

7. Don't keep annoying thoughts bottled up inside you until you explode. Write a letter you don't send, write in a private journal or diary how you feel, or confide in a friend.

8. Understand that you can lose an argument without being a loser.

9. Know that anyone can change. Just keep trying!

10. Keep a sense of humor!

I-20A   SHOULD I OR SHOULDN'T I?

DIRECTIONS FOR THE TEACHER

This game is a modified version of both Tic-Tac-Toe and Bingo to help students recognize the negative influence of a group in order to decide not to participate. It requires the student to first locate, on one of four different game sheets, the situation and decision you read aloud, then to determine whether one should or shouldn't have taken that action.

Players receive one of four game sheets and markers of two different colors. As you read aloud a situation and subsequent action, the players must locate the same situation and action on each of their game sheets. Players decide whether the action *should* or *shouldn't* have been taken. When they have three *shoulds* (vertically, diagonally, horizontally) or three *shouldn'ts* (vertically, diagonally, horizontally), they call out BINGO.

Answer sheet is on next page.

ANSWER SHEET FOR TEACHER

BOARD A

BOARD B

BOARD C

BOARD D

I SHOULD ☐

I SHOULDN'T ▨

Section I: Are You Great in a Group?

SITUATIONS AND DECISIONS

1. Two girls are teasing one.

   You join them.

2. A group tells you that if you play with Mark, they won't be your friends anymore.

   You play with Mark because he is your friend, too.

3. You see some kids putting all the paper towels in the toilet in order to clog it.

   You help them.

4. Someone next to you yells "Booooo. . ." during a music concert in the auditorium.

   You don't like the performance either, but you are quiet.

5. Zach is mimicking everything Remi is saying and doing.

   You think it's funny, but you walk away.

6. Kimberly tells the substitute teacher that it's time for recess.

   You call out, "Yes, the teacher always takes us out at 9:15."

7. After a game in the gym, George blames Sue for losing the game.

   You say to her, "You stink at basketball."

8. The girls tell Claire she smells.

   You quietly make a suggestion to Claire alone, "Just take a shower tonight."

9. You hear a group of kids telling everyone to meet in back of the school at 3:30 because Kiki and Toni are going to fight.

   You tell the teacher.

10. The leader of your group project asks you to act as secretary.

    You refuse. You want to be the leader.

11. Some students are pushing and shoving while in line during a fire drill.

    You decide to push the person in front of you.

12. Two classmates are yelling at each other at recess on the playground. Others have formed a circle around them, shouting, "Fight, fight, fight!"

    You walk away to tell the person in charge.

13. Some kids at a table in the lunchroom are throwing peanuts.

    You pick them up and throw them back.

14. A group of students has been stealing markers from the class collection. Even though you are not part of this group, you know who is involved.

    You do not tell anyone.

I-20C   SHOULD I OR SHOULDN'T I?

BOARD A

Two girls are teasing someone. You join them.	After a game in the gym, George blames Sue for losing the game. You say to her, "You stink at basketball."	The girls tell Claire she smells. You quietly make the suggestion to Claire alone, "Just take a shower tonight."
You see some kids putting all the paper towels in the toilet in order to clog it. You help them.	You hear a group of kids telling everyone to meet in back of the school at 3:30 because Kiki and Toni are going to fight. You tell the teacher.	Someone next to you yells "Booooo . . ." during a music concert in the auditorium. You don't like the performance either, but you are quiet.
The leader of your group project asks you to act as secretary. You refuse. You want to be the leader.	Some students are pushing and shoving while in line during the fire drill. You decide to push the person in front of you.	Two classmates are yelling at each other at recess on the play ground. Others have formed a circle around them, shouting, "Fight, fight, fight!" You walk away to tell the person in charge.

Section I: Are You Great in a Group?

I-20D SHOULD I OR SHOULDN'T I?

BOARD B

A group tells you that if you play with Mark, they won't be your friends anymore. You play with Mark because he's your friend, too.	The girls tell Claire she smells. You quietly make the suggestion to Claire alone, "Just take a shower tonight."	Someone next to you yells "Boooo . . ." during a music concert in the auditorium. You don't like the performance either, but you are quiet.
Kimberly tells the substitute teacher that it's time for recess. You call out, "Yes, the teacher always takes us out at 9:15."	Zack is mimicking everything Remi is saying and doing. You think it's funny. You walk away.	A group of students has been stealing markers from the class collection. Even though you are not part of this group, you know who is involved. You do not tell anyone.
Two girls are teasing someone. You join them.	The leader of your group project asks you to act as secretary. You refuse. You want to be the leader.	Two classmates are yelling at each other at recess on the playground. Others have formed a circle around them, shouting, "Fight, fight, fight!" You walk away to tell the person in charge.

Section I: Are You Great in a Group?

I-20E   SHOULD I OR SHOULDN'T I?

BOARD C

Zack is mimicking everything Remi is saying and doing. You think it's funny. You walk away.	Some kids at a table in the lunchroom are throwing peanuts. You pick them up and throw them back.	You hear a group of kids telling everyone to meet in back of the school at 3:30 because Kiki and Toni are going to fight. You tell the teacher.
The girls tell Claire she smells. You quietly make the suggestion to Claire alone, "Just take a shower tonight."	You see some kids putting all the paper towels in the toilet in order to clog it. You help them.	A group tells you that if you play with Mark, they won't be your friends anymore. You play with Mark because he's your friend, too.
Kimberly tells the substitute teacher that it's time for recess. You call out, "Yes, the teacher always takes us out at 9:15."	After a game in the gym, George blames Sue for losing the game. You say to her, "You stink at basketball."	The leader of your group project asks you to act as secretary. You refuse. You want to be the leader.

I-20F   SHOULD I OR SHOULDN'T I?

BOARD D

After a game in the gym, George blames Sue for losing the game. You say to her, "You stink at basketball."	Two classmates are yelling at each other at recess on the play-ground. Others have formed a circle around them, shouting, "Fight, fight, fight!" You walk away to tell the person in charge.	A group of students has been stealing markers from the class collec-tion. Even though you are not part of this group, you know who is involved. You do not tell anyone.
You see some kids put-ting all the paper towels in the toilet in order to clog it. You help them.	A group tells you that if you play with Mark, they won't be your friends anymore. You play with Mark be-cause he's your friend, too.	Some kids at a table in the lunchroom are throwing peanuts. You pick them up and throw them back.
Someone next to you yells "Booooo . . ." dur-ing a music concert in the auditorium. You don't like the per-formance either, but you are quiet.	You hear a group of kids telling everyone to meet in back of the school at 3:30 because Kiki and Toni are going to fight. You tell the teacher.	Some students are pushing and shoving while in line during the fire drill. You decide to push the person in front of you.

Section I: Are You Great in a Group?

I-21A   DODGING MORE THAN THE BALL!

I-21B   *DODGING MORE THAN THE BALL!*

WHAT ARE THE RULES OF GOOD SPORTSMANSHIP? LIST THEM BELOW.

1. _____
   _____
   _____

2. _____
   _____
   _____

3. _____
   _____

4. _____
   _____

5. _____
   _____

6. _____
   _____

7. _____
   _____

I-21C DODGING MORE THAN THE BALL!

Name _____ Date _____

I-22A   IT'S YOUR BATHROOM!

Names of Students in the Group	List What Is Wrong in This Drawing	How Could You Solve the Problem of Vandalism?
1.	1.	
2.	2.	
3.	3.	
4.	4.	
5.	5.	
	6.	

Section I: Are You Great in a Group?

I-22B   IT'S YOUR BATHROOM!

COMBINED LIST	COMBINED SOLUTIONS

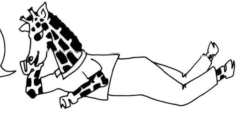

- What is vandalism?
- Why do you think people vandalize?
- What is public property, and how does its vandalism affect all of us?
- How can we stop vandalism in our homes, in our schools, in our community?

- Where have you seen vandalism?
- If you have been a vandal, how have your actions probably affected other people?
- How can you, as an individual, stop vandalism?

Section I: Are You Great in a Group?

Section II

DO YOU VALUE DIVERSITY?

Section II heightens students' awareness of the similarities among all people while acknowledging their differences. Activities cultivate an appreciation for the achievements of racial and ethnic groups; engender respect for religious beliefs, for the elderly and for the interchangeable roles of males and females; and promote empathy for the disabled and for the economically deprived.

Activity/Grade Level/Description

II-1 *The Golden Rule* (K-4) provides students the opportunity to observe illustrations and discuss how kindness begets kindness. Students will then draw, cut, color, and staple to make a booklet.

II-2 *Ask Gramps for Help* (1) begins with a play for students to read and act out. Each student is then invited to recall ways in which an elderly person has enriched his or her life and to write a conversation and act it out using a paper bag puppet as the elderly relative or friend.

II-3 *I Draw, You Run* (2-3) requires you to elicit from students complimentary comments about their peers. Initially, a list of positive qualities (kind, helpful, generous, friendly, cheerful, neat, smart, fair) and talents (jumping rope, drawing, reading, organizing, playing an instrument) may be developed. Then, a writing/drawing activity reinforces the valuable contributions of every student.

II-4 *Even Though I'm Lavender* (3-4) encourages students to accept their differences, respect differences in others, and strive to become the best they can be despite those differences. During discussion accept student responses about their career interests and dreams and encourage the pursuit of these goals. (Refer to activities II-6, "I Am Able Though Disabled" and II-8, "Go Androgynous.")

II-5   *From All Walks of Life* (K-4) demonstrates through anecdotes how real people from varied economic strata have helped others in need. After reading and discussion, ask students to suggest ways in which the class can make a difference.

II-6   *I Am Able Though Disabled* (K-4) fosters the understanding of what it means to be disabled. By participating in a variety of activities, students will experience some of the difficulties faced by people with vision, hearing, learning, developmental, or physical disabilities.

     Use this strategy for the activities pertaining to the hearing disabled. When reading from a big book or giving a spelling test alternately speak clearly, mumble, whisper or just mouth the words. On sheet II-6D there is a rhyme and a paragraph as they would be perceived by the learning disabled. The correct forms follow.

Rhyme
Lucy Locket lost her pocket
Kitty Fisher found it.
There was not a penny in it
Only ribbon around it.

Paragraph
There is a special time each day when the sun
has set and it is not yet night. It is called twilight,
or dusk. It is a time when many creatures who
rest during the day begin to wake.

II-7   *I Can, I Can* (K-4) illustrates the exceptional capabilities of famous disabled people. (Shown are Stevie Wonder, Helen Keller, Itzhak Perlman, and Barbara Jordan.)

II-8   *Go Androgynous* (3-4) invites students of both genders to be receptive of the myriad ways in which they can use their talents and interests. This set of family life/language arts activities promotes an understanding that roles of males and females in today's society are interchangeable and that opportunities abound for success and fulfillment in every avenue of one's life. Here is a list of positive adjectives you may find helpful:

independent	helpful
cheerful	shy
athletic	dramatic
assertive	happy
loyal	strong personality
reliable	has leadership ability
sensitive to the needs	(acts as a leader)
of others	soft spoken
truthful	willing to take risks
understanding	secretive
makes decisions easily	friendly
likeable	gentle
competitive	

II-9 *I Can Speak the Magic Words in Many Languages* (K-4) fosters an appreciation for ethnicity and encourages students to learn and use the "magic" words in 33 languages. It invites students to add any language from their family background.

II-10 *It Could Happen to You* (4) develops an awareness of prejudices involving religion, race, ethnicity, age, poverty, and gender. Suggested questions to begin the discussion are: What is prejudice? How is it different from unfair practice? In what way(s) might *you* be prejudiced?

Take time to read aloud and discuss each of the five scenarios for all that seems wrong. What prejudices does each scenario identify? Why is it sometimes difficult to prove that prejudice exists? Allow students to recall incidences involving true prejudice from their personal experience or that of people they know and write an essay about one such occurrence. Essays may be read aloud and evaluated by peers for plausible prejudice if appropriate.

II-1A   THE GOLDEN RULE

THE GOLDEN RULE IS HELD IN COMMON BY EVERYONE THE WORLD OVER. IT IS THE HIGHEST AND FINEST RULE OF LIFE. THERE ARE MANY WAYS TO STATE IT. HOW IS IT BEING APPLIED IN THESE DRAWINGS?

MY GOLDEN RULE BOOK

(Name)

DO UNTO OTHERS AS YOU WOULD HAVE THEM DO UNTO YOU.

ONE GOOD TURN DESERVES ANOTHER.

KINDNESS BEGETS KINDNESS.

WHAT YOU GIVE TODAY YOU GET TOMORROW.

TREAT PEOPLE THE WAY YOU WANT TO BE TREATED.

II-1B   THE GOLDEN RULE

LOOK AT THE DRAWINGS ON PAGE II-1A. WRITE OR COPY FROM THE BOARD A SIMPLE SENTENCE EXPLAINING HOW EACH ANIMAL IS BEING HELPED. COMPLETE THE LAST TWO BOXES WITH YOUR OWN DRAWINGS SHOWING:
1. HOW YOU HELPED SOMEONE AND
2. HOW YOU WERE HELPED BY SOMEONE ELSE.

MY GOLDEN RULE BOOK **NAME:** _____	 _____ _____
      _____ _____	 _____ _____

II-1C   THE GOLDEN RULE

CUT OUT EACH PICTURE. COLOR THEM IF YOU'D LIKE. PUT THEM IN ORDER. STAPLE THEM TOGETHER TO MAKE YOUR OWN GOLDEN RULE BOOK.

II-2A   ASK GRAMPS FOR HELP

WHEN MY MOM OR DAD ARE TOO BUSY TO PLAY WITH ME I'M GLAD THERE'S GRAMPS. IS THERE AN OLDER PERSON WHO SPENDS TIME PLAYING WITH, READING STORIES TO, OR HELPING YOU? HERE'S A LITTLE PLAY FOR YOU TO READ AND ACT OUT.

"Hi, Gramps! Give me a hug."

"Are you going to stay with me?"

"Hurray! You can read *The Three Bears* with me."

"You sure do make good sandwiches, Gramps."

"When we come back will you play 'Go Fish' with me?"

"I love you, Gramps."

"How's my favorite grandchild?"

"Yup, all afternoon."

"I'll read it out loud while you eat your lunch."

"Thank you. Do you want to go to the park later?"

"Sure."

II-2B   ASK GRAMPS FOR HELP

MAKE A PAPER BAG PUPPET OF AN ELDERLY PERSON WHO LIKES TO SPEND TIME WITH YOU. PUT IT ON YOUR HAND AND HAVE A CONVERSATION WITH YOUR PUPPET ABOUT WHAT YOU LIKE TO DO TOGETHER. YOU CAN WRITE THE CONVERSATION BELOW.

ME: _____

_____

_____

OTHER PERSON: _____

_____

_____

ME: _____

_____

_____

OTHER PERSON: _____

_____

_____

ME: _____

_____

_____

OTHER PERSON: _____

_____

Section II: Do You Value Diversity?

II-3A   I DRAW, YOU RUN

LOOK AT THE LIST OF WORDS THAT YOU AND YOUR TEACHER HAVE MADE ABOUT THE GOOD QUALITIES AND TALENTS THAT YOU AND YOUR CLASSMATES HAVE. WRITE ABOUT A GOOD QUALITY AND A TALENT THAT YOU HAVE.

I like myself whenever I _____

_____

_____

I think I'm good at _____

_____

_____

USE THE SPACE BELOW TO DRAW A PICTURE OF YOURSELF SHOWING SOMETHING YOU DO WELL.

II-3B   I DRAW, YOU RUN

I like _____ because
                    classmate's name

_____

_____

_____ is good at
                    classmate's name

_____

_____

II-4A   EVEN THOUGH I'M LAVENDER

UNDER EACH CATEGORY IN THE CHART BELOW, LIST THE NAMES OF THE GROUPS REPRESENTED BY YOUR CLASSMATES. TOGETHER, ADD OTHERS THAT YOU KNOW ABOUT.

RACES	ETHNIC BACKGROUNDS	DISABILITIES	ECONOMIC STATUSES
		AGE GROUPS	RELIGIONS
GENDERS			

AS YOUR CLASS READS AND DISCUSSES EACH PARAGRAPH ON THE NEXT PAGE, SUBSTITUTE THE WORD "LAVENDER" FOR THE RACE, ETHNIC GROUP, DISABILITY, RELIGION, AGE GROUP, GENDER, ECONOMIC STATUS, OR A COMBINATION THAT DESCRIBE YOU. FOR EXAMPLE, YOU MAY BE A NINE-YEAR-OLD BRAZILIAN INDIAN CATHOLIC PERCEPTUALLY-IMPAIRED GIRL.

Section II: Do You Value Diversity?

THOUGHT #1:   Even though I'm *lavender*, and others have been mean to me, I do not have to be mean to them in return. Two wrongs do not make a right. I will show them by my actions that I am proud of who *I* am and of the way I act.

Questions for Discussion

1. Can you remember a time when one or more members of a group were mean to you because you were different?

2. What is meant by the saying, "Two wrongs do not make a right"?

3. What appropriate responses could you offer to people who treat you badly?

THOUGHT #2:   Even though I am *lavender*, I don't make excuses or blame others for who I am. I try to be the best that I can be. I accept responsibility for my actions and my work.

I am a good student because I try hard, ask for help when I need it, do my assignments, learn good study habits, take suggestions, listen carefully, and participate positively in activities. I deserve to be proud of myself.

Questions for Discussion

1. Have you used your membership in a different group to make excuses for yourself or to blame others?

2. What actions or language would have been better?

3. Why is it important to be a good student?

THOUGHT #3:   People tell me that because I'm *lavender*, I will never be able to have the career I want. I know if I work hard and hold on to my dream, I can succeed and achieve my goal.

Questions for Discussion

1. What would you like to be someday?

2. What do you think you will have to do in order to achieve your goal?

The Caring Institute is a tiny organization that gives national caring awards to well known and little known, wealthy and poor people from every race and region of the country because all of them care for others in some way.

Two brothers, **Bill and Val Halamandaris,** with a handful of workers run this institute. Grandsons of a Greek immigrant who worked on the railroads and sons of a coalminer in Utah, they grew up in a multicultural society where "when somebody needed something, you did what had to be done."

When Val was chosen to go to Washington, D.C. by the American Legion's Boys' Nation Program, he met Utah's Senator Frank Moss who helped both Val and Bill go to college.

Upon graduating from college they could have made a lot of money but instead they went into government service to give back to the people who helped them. After leaving government service, they worked for organizations devoted to improving medical care for the sick and elderly.

In 1985, they founded the Caring Institute. "We were concerned with the materialism of the country and the tremendous amount of attention we were paying to celebrities. There are millions of people doing extraordinary things in this country, and nobody was honoring them.

"We wanted to find people others could admire for both their personal and professional lives."

Anecdotes are reprinted with permission from *Parade,* copyright © 1992.

Section II: Do You Value Diversity?

Bill Halamandaris stated, "We want to remind our country of our tradition of selflessness. We want to bring back the values that have always been fundamental in America."

HERE ARE SOME OF THE PEOPLE WHO HAVE WON THE CARING AWARDS.

Robert Macauley is a businessman who founded AmeriCares, an agency that helps needy people throughout the world.

Henri Landwirth is a hotel owner and self-made millionaire whose Kids Village provides food and rooms for desperately ill children visiting Walt Disney World.

Mary Jo Copeland is a housewife in Minnesota who began her own soup kitchen and feeds the poor.

Alice Harris singlehandedly finds housing for hundreds of homeless neighbors in the Watts neighborhood of Los Angeles. Forty years ago she was a homeless, single teenage mother.

Jerry and Sandy Tucker are a couple with little money who have taken in a houseful of unwanted children.

John Fling is a man from South Carolina who has given everything he has to the poor.

> **Mary Lasker** is a philanthropist who has contributed millions of dollars for medical research and advances in medical care.

Bill Halamandaris highlights the important lesson that winners of the Caring Awards have always known when he says, "There is joy in transcending yourself to serve others."

In 1990, the first Young Adult Caring Awards were presented to youths who had worked with the homeless, organized anti-drug campaigns and AIDS-awareness projects, or made other contributions to their communities. In 1992, the first Caring College Kids Awards were given at schools across the country. In 1991, 60,000 students had entered!

PERHAPS _YOU_ WILL RECEIVE ONE OF THESE AWARDS SOMEDAY.

FROM SECTION 504:   REHABILITATION ACT OF 1973

A DISABILITY MAY BE ANY PHYSICAL OR MENTAL IMPAIRMENT THAT SUBSTANTIALLY IMPAIRS OR RESTRICTS ONE OR MORE MAJOR LIFE ACTIVITIES, SUCH AS CARING FOR ONESELF, PERFORMING MANUAL TASKS, WALKING, SEEING, HEARING, SPEAKING, BREATHING, LEARNING AND WORKING.

WHEN PHYSICAL OR SOCIAL OBSTACLES MAKE IT DIFFICULT FOR PEOPLE TO FULLY PARTICIPATE IN EVERYDAY ENDEAVORS A DISABLED PERSON BECOMES HANDICAPPED.

ELEVATORS WITH NO BRAILLE BUTTONS FOR BLIND PEOPLE, BUILDINGS WITH NO RAMPS FOR WHEELCHAIRS, AND NON-DISABLED PEOPLE WHO ASSUME THAT THE DISABLED WANT HELP ARE EXAMPLES OF THIS.

II-6B   I AM ABLE THOUGH DISABLED

TRY THESE SUGGESTED ACTIVITIES.

VISION DISABLED

- Fill a lunch bag with objects, such as five crayons of the same size and shape but of different colors. Reach into the bag and, without looking, pull out a green crayon. Is this difficult to do? How would a blind person tell the difference among the colors of crayons?

- Make binoculars with your hands and place one hand on each eye. What do you see? What can't you see? Make the binoculars smaller and smaller, and answer the same questions. How could lack of side vision be dangerous for you while performing your everyday activities?

- Hold a three-inch strip of wax paper over your eyes at your temples. Look or walk around the room. What do you see? Is anything clear?

- Get a one-inch letter E from your teacher. Go into the hallway with your classmates. Take turns standing at one end of the hallway while someone posts the one-inch letter E at the other end of the hallway, not going further than 200 feet away or closer than 20 feet away. Where do you have to stand to see the E? A legally blind person would not be able to read the letter E from 20 feet away. That person needs to be ten times closer in order to see it than someone with 20/20 vision.

- Pair up with another student. Take turns being blind-folded (use your own handkerchief or bandana). If you were blind, how would you identify specific books, colored pencils, your own desk, and so on? With a partner, walk around the room while blindfolded. What is it like to be blind? When you are the seeing partner, what are your responsibilities to the person who is blind?

II-6C   I AM ABLE THOUGH DISABLED

HEARING DISABLED

• Listen while the teacher reads from a big book or picture book with text. Listen very carefully to the story because the teacher will call on someone at the end to retell it. Do you have a problem retelling the story? Why? What would help a deaf person understand and enjoy the story?

• Prepare your paper for a spelling test. Listen to the teacher and write the word on your paper. Did you have difficulty spelling all the words? Was it because you didn't know how? Why did you have a problem spelling some of the words?

PHYSICALLY DISABLED

• Using strips of old sheeting or other soft material, have someone tie your hand (left hand if you are lefthanded, right hand if you are righthanded) positioned over your chest or behind your back so that you cannot use it. How difficult do you think your life would be if you could only use one arm and one hand to do everything?

• Tie a block or some other solid, thick object under one shoe. Try walking around the room or down the hallway. How difficult is walking when one foot is shorter than the other?

• Try these three ways of saying your name, address and telephone number: flatten your tongue against the roof of your mouth, flatten your tongue against the bottom of your mouth, flatten your tongue against the bottom of your mouth and place your teeth together. In each instance can you be understood? How difficult is it for someone with a speech problem to communicate?

II-6D I AM ABLE THOUGH DISABLED

LEARNING DISABLED

- Your teacher will pass out a 5" × 7" card or piece of oaktag and a crayon to you. Draw a circle, a square, and a triangle from left to right on one side of the card. Look at the shapes. Now turn the card over and hold it against your forehead with the hand you use to write. Using your other hand, draw a circle, then a square, then a triangle from left to right. When you are finished with all three shapes, compare the two sides of the card. Do the figures look the same? What made this activity difficult?

- Follow the same directions as above, but instead of drawing the three shapes, write the word XANADU. Answer the same questions.

TRY TO READ THIS RHYME.

LUCY LOKCTE LOST HRE BCKET,
KITTY FISHER FOUMBB IT.
THERE SAW MOT A PEMNY IN TI,
OLMY RIPPOM RUOMB IT.

Can you understand what you read? How long did it take to figure out what the words were?

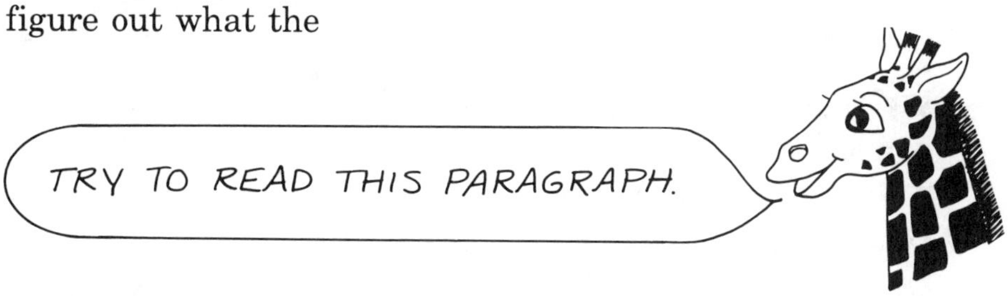
TRY TO READ THIS PARAGRAPH.

TH RE A SPECIAL CH WH E SUN
HAS AND IT IS YET N IT IS D
TW HT, O K. IT MANY ATURES
WHO RE RING T AY BEGI AKE.

Would you understand what you have read if this is what you saw? Discuss the difficulties a person with a learning disability would have with reading and learning something new quickly.

II-6E   I AM ABLE THOUGH DISABLED

DEVELOPMENTALLY DISABLED

- You will play "Simon Says" in a different way. Stand by your seat but give yourself room to move your arms. Rename your head, shoulders, and waist; for example, head = green, shoulders = blue, and waist = red. Follow the teacher's directions while playing the game. What makes this so hard to do at the beginning? Does it become easier when you are given time to concentrate on each direction and have someone to imitate? What do developmentally disabled people need in order to be successful at a task?

SIMON SAYS, HANDS ON GREEN.

- Decide on something simple to make in the classroom with a piece of paper, such as a square from a rectangle, a paper airplane, and so on. Take turns giving directions to a classmate or select someone to give directions to the whole class. Were the directions clear? Did the person giving the directions speak slowly, going step by step so you could follow them? Did you understand the directions? Were you able to make the object and did it look good by following the directions? What are some of the ways you could help a developmentally disabled person learn something new?

TIPS FOR THOUGHTFUL BEHAVIOR WITH DISABLED PERSONS

- Ask if help is needed before helping, or wait until you are asked for help.

- You may ask questions, but don't expect answers about a person's disability.

ARE THERE ANY THOUGHTFUL TIPS YOU CAN ADD TO THIS LIST?

- Someone using a wheelchair is not necessarily sick or weak.

- When speaking with a disabled person, don't avoid words like walk, run, see, hear.

- Blind people are not deaf. Don't yell!

- Seeing Eye dogs have an important job. Don't pet them.

- When you invite disabled friends out or to your home, make them feel comfortable, included, and safe.

- Handicapped parking spaces are reserved for people with disabilities. Don't let your parents park there, unless, of course, they are handicapped.

- Treat a disabled person the way you would want to be treated.

II-7   I CAN, I CAN

DO YOU RECOGNIZE ANY OF THE PEOPLE BELOW? WHAT ARE THEY KNOWN FOR DOING? DO YOU KNOW ANY OTHER FAMOUS PEOPLE WHO ARE DISABLED?

Section II: Do You Value Diversity?

II-8A GO ANDROGYNOUS

STUDY EACH DRAWING. IS THERE ANYTHING UNUSUAL ABOUT A GIRL PLAYING FOOTBALL OR A MAN IRONING? WHY AND WHY NOT? USE A DICTIONARY TO FIND THE MEANING OF THE WORD "ANDROGYNOUS."

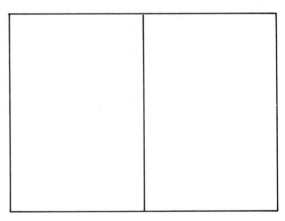

NOW LIST ON THE BOARD AT LEAST 20 ADJECTIVES THAT DESCRIBE HUMAN QUALITIES, LIKE "AFFECTIONATE," "FORCEFUL," "TACTFUL," ETC. THEN GO BACK TO EACH ADJECTIVE AND DISCUSS WHETHER IT MOSTLY DESCRIBES MALES, MOSTLY DESCRIBES FEMALES, OR IS TRUE FOR BOTH.

Section II: Do You Value Diversity?

II-8B   GO ANDROGYNOUS

LOOK AT THE LIST OF SPORTS. CIRCLE THE SPORTS IN WHICH YOU ENJOY PARTICIPATING. UNDERLINE THE ONES YOU LIKE TO WATCH NOW AND MIGHT LIKE TO PARTICIPATE IN SOMEDAY.

Aerobics	Go-cart racing	Running
Archery	Golfing	Skateboarding
Baseball	Gymnastics	Skating, ice
Basketball	Hiking	Skating, roller
Bike riding	Hockey, field	Skiing, cross country
Boating	Hockey, ice	Skiing, downhill
Bowling	Horseback riding	Soccer
Boxing	Hunting	Swimming
Car racing	Jogging	Tennis
Croquet	Karate	Tobogganing
Dancing	Lacrosse	Track
Dirt biking	Moped riding	Volleyball
Diving	Motorcycling	Walking
Fishing	Paddle tennis	White water rafting
Flying	Pingpong	Wrestling
Football	Polo	_____
	Pool (billiards)	_____

READ YOUR FAVORITE SPORTS TO YOUR CLASSMATES AND LISTEN TO THEIR'S. HOW OFTEN WAS A SPORT CHOSEN BY BOYS AND GIRLS?

Section II: Do You Value Diversity?

II-8C   GO ANDROGYNOUS

HERE IS A LIST OF ACTIVITIES AND HOBBIES. CIRCLE THE ONES YOU DO. UNDERLINE THOSE THAT YOU MIGHT LIKE TO DO SOMEDAY.

Painting	Chess
Drawing	Checkers
Crocheting	Other board games
Knitting	Computer games
Sewing	Building things
Stitchery	Collecting things
Weaving	Cooking
Woodworking	Baking
Embroidery	Reading
Needlepoint	Playing an instrument
Singing	Gardening
Writing	Dramatics
Sightseeing	Boating
Amusement park rides	Projects to earn money
Concerts	Travel
Picnicking	Sports
Puzzles	Foreign languages
Card games	Science experiments

_____   _____

_____   _____

READ YOUR CHOICES ALOUD TO YOUR CLASSMATES AND LISTEN AS THEY READ THEIR OWN. HOW MANY TIMES WERE THE SAME HOBBIES AND ACTIVITIES CHOSEN BY BOTH GIRLS AND BOYS IN YOUR CLASS?

Section II: Do You Value Diversity?

II-8D   GO ANDROGYNOUS

READ THE LISTS OF SAMPLE OCCUPATIONS ON THIS PAGE AND THE NEXT. WHICH ONE DO YOU KNOW SOMETHING ABOUT? LOOK THROUGH NEWSPAPERS AND MAGAZINES, LISTEN TO TV AND RADIO AND GET HELP FROM ADULTS IN ORDER TO ADD TO THE LISTS.

Agriculture
farmer
meat packer
butcher
produce manager
horticulturist
   etc.

Arts
orchestra conductor
dancer
sculptor
curator
actor/actress
   etc.

Business
secretary
CEO (chief executive officer)
entrepreneur
bookkeeper
stockperson
   etc.

Communications
computer programmer
telephone operator
TV anchorperson
postmaster general
newspaper reporter
   etc.

Construction
mason
electrician
architect
plumber
carpenter
   etc.

Education
librarian
teacher
principal
commissioner
aide
   etc.

Entertainment
singer
scriptwriter
film editor
make-up artist
comedian
   etc.

Finance
stockbroker
banker
accountant
analyst
teller
   etc.

Law
judge
lawyer
clerk
court stenographer
baliff
   etc.

Maintenance
custodian
mechanic
shoe repairperson
landscaper
roofer
   etc.

II-8D   GO ANDROGYNOUS (CONTINUED)

Manufacturing
assembly line worker
foreman
union leader
wholesaler
miner
etc.

Medicine
doctor
nurse
technician
physical therapist
psychiatrist
etc.

Military
naval commander
sergeant
general
etc.

Politics/Government
mayor
governor
IRS auditor
council member
sheriff
etc.

Religion
priest
rabbi
choirmaster
deacon
minister
nun
etc.

Science/Math
inventor
researcher
botanist
engineer
archaeologist
etc.

Service
waiter/waitress
steward/stewardess
beautician
butler
salesperson
etc.

Social Service
social worker
police officer
nursing home director
firefighter
paramedic
etc.

Sports
jockey
professional player
coach
umpire
professional ice skater
etc.

Transportation
dispatcher
ship captain
airline pilot
truck driver
air traffic controller
etc.

Name _____ **Date** _____

II-8E   GO ANDROGYNOUS

USE THIS INTERVIEW SHEET TO QUESTION AN ADULT ABOUT HIS OR HER OCCUPATION. COLLECT DETAILED INFORMATION.

INTERVIEW SHEET

Name of person being interviewed: _____

Occupation: _____

1. What training and/or education was necessary for you to get your job? _____

_____

2. What are your responsibilities? _____

_____

3. What do you enjoy most about your job? _____

_____

4. What is difficult about the job? _____

_____

5. Do you see this job as your lifetime career? Why or why not? _____

_____

6. Is this a job that either a man or a woman could perform? Why or why not? _____

_____

7. Is there any other job you would like to do? Why? _____

_____

II-8F GO ANDROGYNOUS

MAKE A SHORT SPEECH ABOUT THE JOB INFORMATION IN YOUR INTERVIEW. WRITE KEY WORDS AND PHRASES ON THIS NOTE CARD. PRACTICE SAYING THE INFORMATION IN SENTENCE FORM AT HOME SEVERAL TIMES BEFORE THE DAY OF YOUR PRESENTATION.

PRESENTER'S NOTECARD

Name of person interviewed: _____

Occupation: _____

Training/education: _____

Responsibilities: _____

_____

Job likes and dislikes: _____

_____

Job for either gender? Why or why not? _____

_____

_____

– – – – – – – – – – – – – TEAR OFF – – – – – – – – – – – – –

PRESENTER'S NOTECARD

Name of person interviewed: _____

Occupation: _____

Training/education: _____

Responsibilities: _____

_____

Job likes and dislikes: _____

_____

Job for either gender? Why or why not? _____

_____

_____

Section II: Do You Value Diversity?

II-8G   GO ANDROGYNOUS

USE THIS FORM TO CRITIQUE A CLASSMATE'S SPEECH.
THEN GIVE IT TO THE SPEAKER TO READ AND KEEP.

Name of presenter: _____

1. **CONTENT:** How complete was the information?   EXCELLENT   GOOD   FAIR   POOR

2. **ORGANIZATION:** Did the ideas follow a logical order?   EXCELLENT   GOOD   FAIR   POOR

3. **FLOW OF ORAL LANGUAGE:** Did sentence follow sentence in a smooth and steady manner?   EXCELLENT   GOOD   FAIR   POOR

4. **EYE CONTACT:** Did the speaker look at the audience more than at the notecard?   EXCELLENT   GOOD   FAIR   POOR

5. **VOLUME AND CLARITY:** Could you understand every word?   EXCELLENT   GOOD   FAIR   POOR

— — — — — — — — — — — — — TEAR OFF — — — — — — — — — — — —

Name of presenter: _____

1. **CONTENT:** How complete was the information?   EXCELLENT   GOOD   FAIR   POOR

2. **ORGANIZATION:** Did the ideas follow a logical order?   EXCELLENT   GOOD   FAIR   POOR

3. **FLOW OF ORAL LANGUAGE:** Did sentence follow sentence in a smooth and steady manner?   EXCELLENT   GOOD   FAIR   POOR

4. **EYE CONTACT:** Did the speaker look at the audience more than at the notecard?   EXCELLENT   GOOD   FAIR   POOR

5. **VOLUME AND CLARITY:** Could you understand every word?   EXCELLENT   GOOD   FAIR   POOR

Section II: Do You Value Diversity?

Did you know that more than 100 languages are spoken around the world? Although the words are different, the meanings are very often the same.

On the next three pages you'll find "good morning," "please," "thank you," "goodbye," and "you're welcome" in 33 languages.

What is the language of *your* ancestors? By asking an authority or listening to a cassette, find out how to pronounce these "magic" words and substitute them for their English translations in class.

II-9B I CAN SPEAK THE MAGIC WORDS IN MANY LANGUAGES

"MAGIC" PHRASES AND WORDS

LANGUAGE	Good morning	Please	Thank you	Good-bye	You're welcome
ENGLISH	Good morning	Please	Thank you	Good-bye	You're welcome
ARABIC	'Fil wasaτ	Min 'fadhlak	Mash kuur	—	'Eafwan
BULGARIAN	Dobro' oo' teo	Mo' lya	Dobre' sum	Dovi' zhdane	—
CHINESE, CANTONESE	Jo sun	Ching nay	Daw jeah nay	Joy geen	—
CHINESE, MANDARIN	Džău-ǎn	Chĭng	Syèsye nĭ	Dzái jyan	Bú kèchi
CZECH	Dobrý' den	Prosím	Děkuji vám	Na shledanou	Prosím
DANISH	God morgen	Vær sagod	Tak	Farvel	Vær sǻgod
DUTCH	Goede morgen	Als 't u blieft	Dank u	Tot ziens	Geen dank
FARSI (Persian)	Salām (Hello)	Lotfan	Mamnoon am	Khodä Häfez	Ghäbel nadäreh
FINNISH	Huomenta	Ole hyvä	Kiitos	Näkemiin	Olkaa hyvä
FRENCH	Bonjour	S'il vous plaît	Merci	Au révoir	Il nỳ a pas de quoi
GERMAN	Gut morgen	Bitte	Danke schön	Auf wiedersehen	Bitte sehr
GREEK	Kale méra	Parakaló	Efkharistó	Adéo	Parakaló

Section II: Do You Value Diversity?

II-9C   I CAN SPEAK THE MAGIC WORDS IN MANY LANGUAGES

"MAGIC" PHRASES AND WORDS

LANGUAGE					
HINDI	Nam ás tee	Kripayáa	Dhányavaad	Namástee	Kóoii báat nahii
HUNGARIAN	Jóreggelt	Kérem	Jól vagyok	Viszontlátásra	Szívesen
INDONESIAN	Selamat pagi	Silahkan	Terima kasih	Selamat djalan	Terima kasih kembali
IRISH (GAELIC)	Jeeahgwitch (Hello)	Led hell	Guh row mow ught	Slawn laht	Thaw fawlt chew row at
ITALIAN	Buon giorno	Per favore	Grazie	Arrivederci	Prego
JAPANESE	Ohayo gozaimasu	Dozo	Arigato gozaimasu	Sayonara	Do itashimashite
KOREAN	Anny ônghi chumusôtsupnikka	—	Komapsûphida	Anny ônghi kasipsiyo	Won ch' ônmaneyo
NORWEGIAN	God morgen	Takk	Tusen takk	Farvel	Ingen årsak
POLISH	Dzien' dobry panu	Prozę	Dz iękuję	Dowidzenia	Prozę bardzo
PORTUGUESE	Bom dia	Por favor	Obrigado(a)	Adeus	Não há de que
ROMANIAN	Bună dimieeța	Vă rog	Mulțumesc	La revedere	——
RUSSIAN	Dobroyeh oot-ro	Pozhaloosta	Spaseeba	Proschchayteh	Niehzachto

Section II: Do You Value Diversity?

II-9D   I CAN SPEAK THE MAGIC WORDS IN MANY LANGUAGES

LANGUAGE	"MAGIC" PHRASES AND WORDS				
SERBO-CROATIAN	Dobro jutro	Molim	Huala	Do vidjenja	Izvolite
SPANISH	Buenas días	Por favor	Gracias	Adiós	De Nada
SWAHILI	Hu j ambo	T afadhali	Asanta sana	Kwa heri	Si kitu
SWEDISH	God morgon	Var så god	Tack	Adj ö	Ingen orsak
TAGALOG (Philipino)	Magandáng umága sa inuo	Pkisuyò	Maraming	—	Walang anó man
THAI	Swatdee	Karuna	Khob khun krub	Swatdee ka	Mai pen rai ka
TURKISH	Merhba (*Hello*)	Lûtfen	Iyiyim	Güle güle	—
VIETNAMESE	Tyào	Xinn âumg làm ðn	Cám on âumg	Tyào âumg	Tôy khâumg yám
WELSH	Bore da	Os gwelwch yn dda	Diolch i chi	Da boch	Croeso

Section II: Do You Value Diversity?

II-10   IT COULD HAPPEN TO YOU

EACH STORY INVOLVES PREJUDICE. AS YOU READ TRY TO DISCOVER WHAT'S WRONG.

Harry, a black boy, Charles, a Chinese boy, and James, a white boy, were in gym class shooting baskets. Charles took the ball away from Harry, which made Harry angry. He pushed Charles and made a racial slur. James, who was Harry's best friend, punched Charles and continued to taunt him with the racial slur.

WHAT'S WRONG HERE?

Mr. Samson's class is preparing the room for a birthday party. Kathy has brought cupcakes and juice. Reeza has to leave the classroom before the party begins. The teacher explains that her religious beliefs do not allow her to participate. One of the students calls out, "What a stupid religion that is!"

WHAT'S WRONG HERE?

Jennifer, Paula, Idalia, Rhoda, and Anna were walking home behind an old woman with a cane. Paula whispered to the girls to start running and bump into her. The woman fell down, and the girls ran away laughing.

WHAT'S WRONG HERE?

Everyone in the class made fun of George because, even though his clothes were clean, they had holes in them. The week it turned very cold George was absent because he didn't have a warm jacket. Most of the students were annoyed that George stayed home while they had to be in school working.

WHAT'S WRONG HERE?

The class was talking about the jobs their parents had. Ruth said, "My mom drives a delivery truck." Peter laughed and said, "Your mom drives a truck? That's a man's job!"

WHAT'S WRONG HERE?

Section III

ARE YOU A FRIENDLY FRIEND?

Section III makes students aware of the qualities needed in order to be a friend, make a friend, and keep a friend.

Activity/Grade Level/Description

III-1 *Let's Take Turns* (K) is a brief puppet show presented by the teacher. The discussion that follows needs to elicit ideas about how friends should act with each other when *sharing*. Suggested questions are: (1) What happened here? (2) What is the problem? (3) How can Unfair Unger and Fighting Fiona solve their problem?

III-2 *Winning and Losing* (1) is another brief puppet show presented by the teacher. The discussion that follows needs to elicit ideas about how friends should act with each other when *playing games*. Suggested questions are: (1) What happened here? (2) What is the problem? (3) How can Cheating Charlie and Whining Winona be better winners and losers?

III-3 *Kind or Hurtful?* (K-4) is a finger puppet show created and performed by students. Conversations should reflect the students' own experiences using the character names listed or others.

III-4 *Code of Friendship* (2-3) is a decoding activity whose message is "In order to make a friend, I need to be a friend."

III-5 *Is This Any Way to Treat a Friend?* (2-4) pairs students to answer the questions about how each has been treated by his or her friends. Then the class is reconvened as a whole to graph the responses.

III-6 *Be a Friend, Make a Friend* (2-4) is a brainstorming activity for small groups to follow and reinforce *Code of Friendship* or *Is This Any Way to Treat a Friend?* Divide the class into groups of three to five with a secretary and one copy of the activity sheet. After 10 minutes, meet as a whole class to share the results.

III-7 *Abundant, Affable Adjectives* (4) is geared to expand the students' vocabulary as they find positive characteristics in the thesaurus to describe a true friend. Make sure students select suitable adjectives. As a follow-up, have students locate "amusing" (for example, daffy, dilapidated) or "negative" (for example, deceitful, demeaning) adjectives. Students who have difficulty with this activity could find the meanings of these words in a dictionary:

F   faithful, forgiving

R   reasonable, reliable

I   interesting, insightful

E   energetic, encouraging

N   nice, normal

D   decent, delightful

L   likeable, level-headed

Y   youthful, yeomanly

F   frank, fun-loving

R   resourceful, respectful

I   imaginative, impartial

E   easygoing, everlasting

N   nurturing, neighborly

D   dependable, discreet

III-1A LET'S TAKE TURNS

UNGER AND FIONA ARE FRIENDS. THEY ARE ON THE PLAYGROUND WITH FIONA'S SCOOTER. BOTH WANT TO RIDE IT.

WATCH THE PUPPET SHOW THAT YOUR TEACHER PUTS ON. BE READY TO TALK ABOUT THE UNFRIENDLY THINGS THAT UNFAIR UNGER AND FIGHTING FIONA ARE SAYING AND DOING.

THE SCRIPT

UNFAIR UNGER	FIGHTING FIONA
May I ride your scooter?	No!
Why not?	Because you never give it back.
Yes, I do!	You do not! How about yesterday when I let you ride it and you took it down the block and left it there?
So. You went and got it.	But I had to walk down the street to look for it.
(*Unger pushes Fiona.*)	Stop pushing me or you'll never get it again. (*Fiona hits Unger.*)
Stop it! Your mother said I could ride it.	I don't care. It's mine.

III-1B LET'S TAKE TURNS

III-1C   LET'S TAKE TURNS

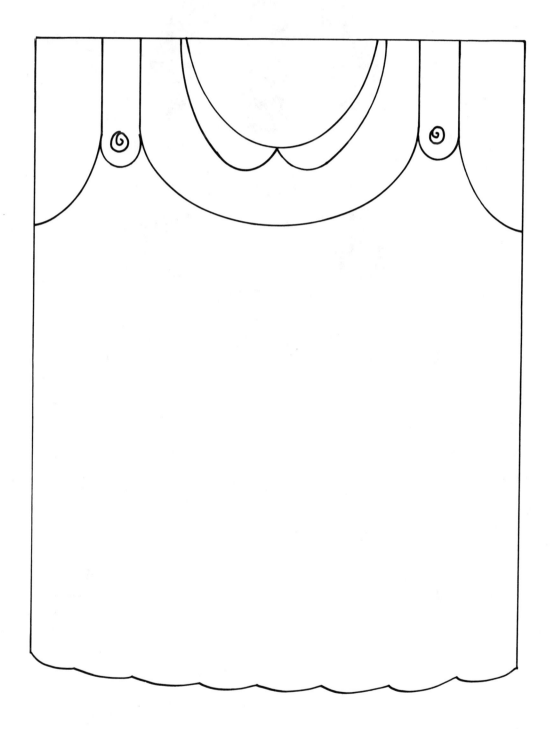

III-1D   LET'S TAKE TURNS

III-1E   LET'S TAKE TURNS

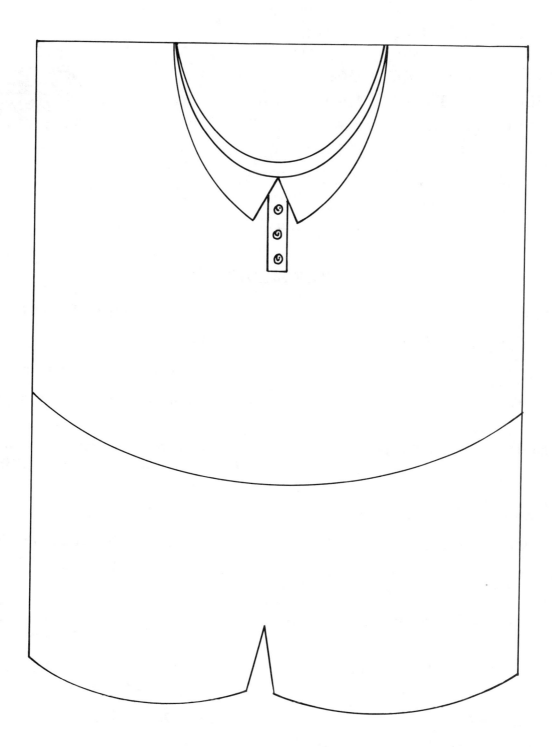

III-2A WINNING AND LOSING

CHEATING CHARLIE AND WHINING WINONA ARE FRIENDS. THEY ARE PLAYING A BOARD GAME CALLED "MOUNTAIN TOP." BOTH WANT TO WIN.

WATCH THE PUPPET SHOW THAT YOUR TEACHER PUTS ON. BE READY TO TALK ABOUT CHARLIE AND WINONA'S UNFRIENDLY BEHAVIOR.

THE SCRIPT

CHEATING CHARLIE	WHINING WINONA
Wanna play "Mountain Top"?	O.K.
I'll go first.	You went first the last time.
Let's shake the dice.	You have a seven. I'm going to get more.
You got three. I start the game.	It's not fair. I dropped it. I'm doing it over again. Now it's ten.
You have three! I go first.	Oh, go ahead.
Five. I move five spaces.	You moved six. That's cheating!
I did not!	Look. You were there. One, two, three, four, five. See?
It was just a little mistake.	It's my turn to pick a card. Wow! I'm way ahead. I'm gonna win!
My dice say twelve. Ha, ha, ha, ha, ha.	So what! It's only a game. Oh, no! I hate this card.
Now I'm ahead.	It's not fair. I quit!
Oh stop crying, you big baby.	

Name _____ Date _____

III-2B   WINNING AND LOSING

III-2C   WINNING AND LOSING

III-2D   WINNING AND LOSING

III-2E   WINNING AND LOSING

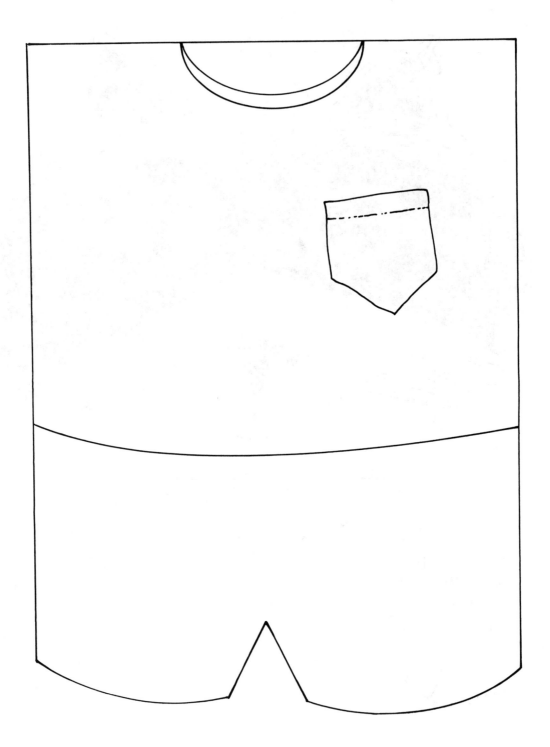

Name _____ Date _____

III-3   KIND OR HURTFUL?

Directions:
_____

Cut out the finger puppets, add a
face, hair, etc., and put them on a
finger of each hand. Choose a
name for each puppet and make
up a conversation the two might
have about being a Friendly
Friend.

Possible puppet names:
_____

Obnoxious Ollie
Kind Ken
Atrocious Al
Thoughtful Thelma
Mean Minnie
Considerate Cary
Hurtful Harry
Tactful Tess
Sarcastic Sarah
Decent Debbie

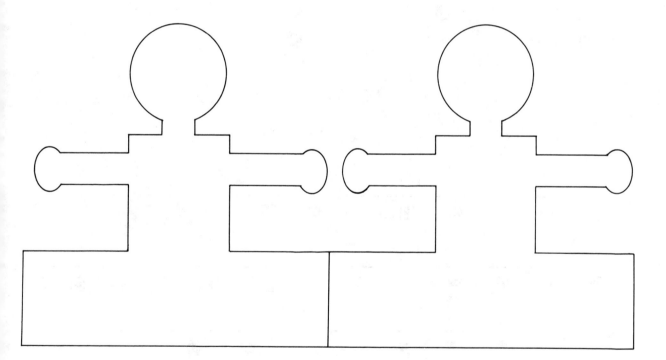

USING THE ALPHABET BELOW, DECIPHER THIS IMPORTANT MESSAGE.

O = A   ◉ = H   = O   ◈ = V
▼ = B   ◇ = I   ◖ = P   ➡ = W
■ = C   ▲ = J   Ø = Q   ⊖ = X
⇨ = D   ◬ = K   ▯ = R   ☐ = Y
▬ = E   ▭ = L   ⇦ = S   ● = Z
△ = F   ◐ = M   ◆ = T
◀ = G   ⊡ = N   ◎ = U

MESSAGE

IN ORDER TO

MAKE A FRIEND,

I NEED TO BE

A FRIEND.

III-5   IS THIS ANY WAY TO TREAT A FRIEND?

1. Has a friend ever tried to keep you from having another friend?

2. Has a friend ever made fun of you to someone else?

3. Has a friend ever lied to you?

4. Has a friend ever lied about you?

5. Has a friend told someone else a secret of yours?

Name:	Name:
Q. 1 Yes No	Q. 1 Yes No
Q. 2 Yes No	Q. 2 Yes No
Q. 3 Yes No	Q. 3 Yes No
Q. 4 Yes No	Q. 4 Yes No
Q. 5 Yes No	Q. 5 Yes No

NUMBER OF YES RESPONSES IN THE CLASS

	27					
	26					
	25					
	24					
	23					
	22					
	21					
	20					
	19					
	18					
	17					
	16					
	15					
	14					
	13					
	12					
	11					
	10					
	9					
	8					
	7					
	6					
	5					
	4					
	3					
	2					
	1					
QUESTIONS		1	2	3	4	5

III-6   BE A FRIEND, MAKE A FRIEND

IN ORDER TO
<u>MAKE</u> A FRIEND,
YOU HAVE TO <u>BE</u> A FRIEND.
HOW DO YOU THINK YOU
SHOULD ACT TOWARDS
A FRIEND?

DIRECTIONS:
LIST THE WAYS
BELOW.
EXAMPLE: <u>A FRIEND
IS NOT BOSSY.</u>

A friend _____

A friend _____

A friend _____

A friend _____

A friend _____

A friend _____

A friend _____

A friend _____

A friend _____

A friend _____

III-7 ABUNDANT, AFFABLE ADJECTIVES

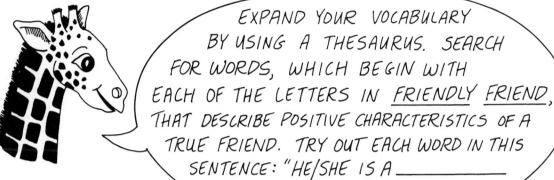

EXPAND YOUR VOCABULARY BY USING A THESAURUS. SEARCH FOR WORDS, WHICH BEGIN WITH EACH OF THE LETTERS IN <u>FRIENDLY FRIEND</u>, THAT DESCRIBE POSITIVE CHARACTERISTICS OF A TRUE FRIEND. TRY OUT EACH WORD IN THIS SENTENCE: "HE/SHE IS A _____ FRIEND," BEFORE WRITING IT BELOW. AN EXAMPLE WOULD BE <u>DESIRABLE</u> FOR THE LETTER <u>D</u>.

F _____

R _____

I _____

E _____

N _____

D _____

L _____

Y _____

F _____

R _____

I _____

E _____

N _____

D _____

Section IV

ARE YOU A TACTFUL TALKER?

This section teaches students some of the thoughtful, respectful, and considerate language required every day of people working, playing, and living together in a society.

Activity/Grade Level/Description

IV-1   *What Do You Say, Dear?* (K-4) reinforces the use of "magic words." First, list the magic words on the board and discuss their many appropriate uses with the class. Then distribute pages IV-1A through IV-1E, which pertain to the creation of an accordion booklet about the magic words. (Directions are included.) Pages IV-1F and IV-1G may be used by you to tally the magic words you hear each student say during one week. Page IV-1H is a certificate that can be presented at the end of that week to each student who successfully incorporated magic words into his or her classroom conversation.

IV-2   *I'd Like You to Meet . . .* (2-4) teaches students to make introductions prior to an open house, a subject fair, a moving-up ceremony, or any other event to be attended by students, their family members, other visitors, and the school staff, most of whom will converse more comfortably after having been properly introduced.

Second-grade teachers may wish to omit page IV-2B and explain its contents more simply to the class. Third- and fourth-grade teachers should hold distribution of page IV-2B until their students have had time to analyze the four scenes on page IV-2A and arrive at one or more rules. As a follow-up, groups of three children each can role play hypothetical introductions for the rest of the class to evaluate.

IV-3   *The Foot-in-Mouth Game* (2-4) invites students to replace tact*less* conversation with tact*ful* conversation. Explain to the group that "to put your foot in your mouth" is an expression that means you said something to cause yourself and your listeners embarrassment. Then have the students read and follow the directions printed on the activity sheet.

IV-4   *What Should I Say Now?* (**3-4**) presents students with a dozen social situations they've probably encountered but for which they've not yet learned a diplomatic or sensitive response. Two possible choices follow each scenario: one is an impetuous, rude and hurtful remark that many children will recognize; the other, the preferred alternative, is well thought out, polite and much more likely to engender continued good feeling.

IV-1A WHAT DO YOU SAY, DEAR?

THE WORDS SHOOTING OUT OF THE MAGICIAN'S HAT ARE CALLED MAGIC WORDS BECAUSE GOOD FEELINGS HAPPEN—LIKE MAGIC—WHEN WE USE THEM.

DIRECTIONS FOR MAKING A MAGIC WORDS ACCORDION BOOKLET

FIRST: Talk with your classmates about *when* each magic word or phrase should be used.

SECOND: Draw one of the ways you talked about on each page that has a bubble. You will make seven drawings. Put two people or animals in each picture.

THIRD: Cut on the bold lines.

FOURTH: Follow the directions on the flaps for gluing and folding.

FIFTH: On page nine, make a tally mark every time you *say* a magic word in school. After one week, total your tally marks.

IV-1B   WHAT DO YOU SAY, DEAR?

GLUE THIS FLAP IN BACK OF PAGE FOUR. FOLD ON THE DOTTED LINES.

GOOD-BYE!

PAGE THREE

HELLO!

PAGE TWO

Name _____ **Date** _____

IV-1C *WHAT DO YOU SAY, DEAR?*

GLUE THIS FLAP IN BACK OF PAGE SIX. FOLD ON THE DOTTED LINES.

THANK YOU....

PAGE FIVE

PLEASE...

PAGE FOUR

Section IV: Are You a Tactful Talker?

IV-1D WHAT DO YOU SAY, DEAR?

GLUE THIS FLAP IN BACK OF PAGE EIGHT. FOLD ON THE DOTTED LINES.

I'M SORRY!

PAGE SEVEN

YOU'RE WELCOME!

PAGE SIX

IV-1E   WHAT DO YOU SAY, DEAR?

MAGIC WORD TALLY

HELLO	GOOD-BYE	PLEASE	THANK YOU	YOU'RE WELCOME	I'M SORRY	EXCUSE ME	TOTAL AT END OF WEEK

PAGE NINE

EXCUSE ME!

PAGE EIGHT

IV-1F   *WHAT DO YOU SAY, DEAR?*

NAME	MAGIC WORD TALLY

CUT HERE AND ATTACH TO TOP OF TALLY PORTION OF THE
NEXT PAGE.

Section IV: Are You a Tactful Talker?

IV-1G   *WHAT DO YOU SAY, DEAR?*

CUT HERE AND ATTACH TO COPY(IES) OF THIS SHEET.

YOU'RE MAGICAL!

NAME _____

IV-2A   I'D LIKE YOU TO MEET . . .

SCENE ONE

SCENE TWO

SCENE THREE

SCENE FOUR

IV-2B   I'D LIKE YOU TO MEET . . .

HERE ARE THE ANSWERS. HOW WELL DID YOU DO?

In SCENE ONE Ms. Giraffe was mentioned first because she is older than Chee Chee Chimp. <u>Young people are introduced to older people.</u>

In SCENE TWO Ms. Giraffe was mentioned first because she is female while Mr. Chimp is male. <u>Gentlemen are introduced to ladies.</u>

In SCENE THREE Mr. Chimp was mentioned first because he is older than Gerry Giraffe. It does not matter that Mr. Chimp is male and Gerry is female, here. <u>Young people are introduced to older people.</u>

In SCENE FOUR Mayor Chimp is mentioned first because his social standing or rank is higher than that of Ms. Giraffe, a teacher. <u>A lower-ranking person is introduced to a higher-ranking person no matter what the age or gender.</u>

NOW YOU TRY. WRITE THE FOLLOWING INTRODUCTIONS AS QUOTATIONS.

INTRODUCE:

1. Your mother to your teacher.
2. Your friend to your mother.
3. Your male cousin to your female friend.
4. Your dad to your dentist.
5. The delivery boy to your grandfather.
6. Your friend's mother to your grandmother.
7. Your older sister to the superintendent of schools.
8. Your friend to another friend of the same age.

IV-3A   THE FOOT-IN-MOUTH GAME

EVERYONE
WINS WITH
TACTFUL TALK!

DIRECTIONS

Two people play this game. Both are winners if, at the end, all boxes on the gameboard are covered with the correct tactful talk you see in the rectangles below. So read carefully! To play, cut out the rectangles on this page. Turn them over and mix them up. Take turns picking up one at a time, reading it and deciding which "tactless talk" to cover on the gameboard. It's okay to change your mind as you go along. Proofread everything when you have finished.

HARRY, MAY I SEE YOU FOR A MINUTE?	EXCUSE ME. THIS ANSWER LOOKS RIGHT.	LET'S SIT DOWN TOGETHER.
I'LL CHECK YOUR ANSWER TO SEE IF I'VE MADE A MISTAKE.	LET'S TALK RIGHT AFTER SCHOOL.	THANK YOU. HE'LL BE THERE IN A MINUTE.

EXCUSE ME. JACK'S DAD IS HERE TO TAKE HIM TO THE DENTIST.	MR. SMITH, COULD I SEE YOU PRIVATELY?	I DON'T UNDERSTAND THIS MATH. COULD YOU HELP ME?	YES, MS. SMITH.

Section IV: Are You a Tactful Talker?

IV-3B THE FOOT-IN-MOUTH GAME

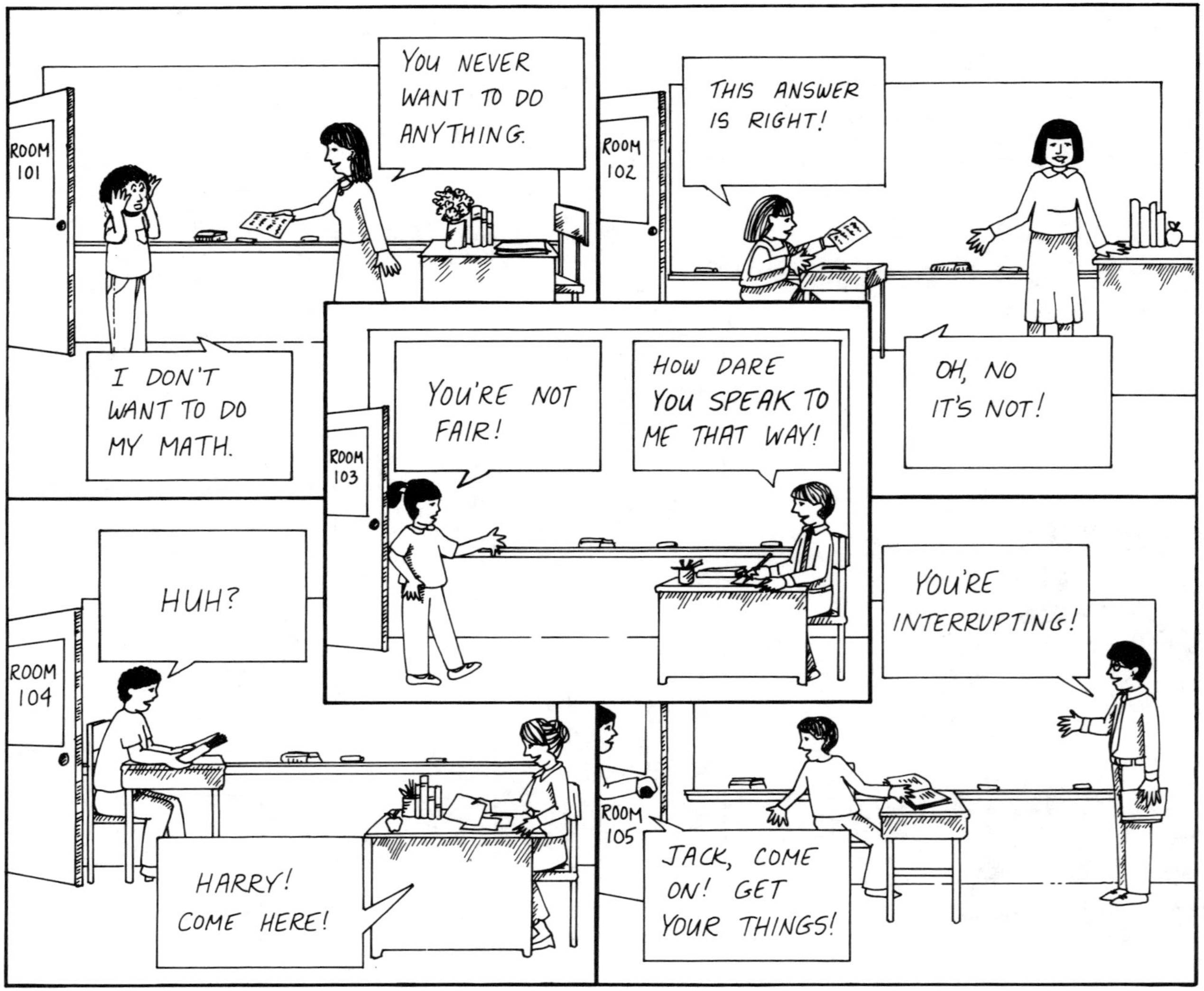

IV-4A   WHAT SHOULD I SAY, NOW?

CIRCLE THE BETTER RESPONSE IN EACH BOX.

AT THE BOTTOM OF THE NEXT PAGE, WORK WITH A CLASSMATE TO CREATE TWO ANECDOTES OF YOUR OWN.

I dialed the wrong number. A strange voice answers the phone. I say,
  a. "I'm sorry, I dialed the wrong number."
  b. "Who's this?"
	Someone called our house and asked for Sue. They had the wrong number. I answered,
	  a. "Wrong number, dummy."
	  b. "I'm sorry, you have the wrong number."

As my friends were leaving my birthday party,
  a. I called from the dining room, "Bye."
  b. I walked them to the door and said, "Thank you for coming. I hope you had a good time."
	While opening a present at my party, I said,
	  a. "Thank you, this is very nice."
	  b. "Ugh, I already have one of these."

I was waiting at the souvenir counter with some other people. When my turn came, someone barged in front of me. I said,
  a. "Excuse me, I think it's my turn."
  b. "Hey, I was first."
	At the movies the person in front of me began to talk loudly during the film. I said,
	  a. "Shut up!"
	  b. "Excuse me, could you please stop talking. I can't hear."

IV-4B   WHAT SHOULD I SAY, NOW?

In class while I was trying to concentrate on my work, someone was making loud tapping noises with his/her pencil. I said,
 	
    a. "Would you cut that out!"
    b. "Please stop that. I'm trying to concentrate."
	I was upset with the grade I got in science and thought it was not right. I went to the teacher and said,
	
	    a. "Would you please check this mark again? I don't understand why I didn't do better."
	    b. "This grade isn't fair!"

A classmate called and asked me to come over to play. This classmate is a bully and I don't want to go over. I say,
 	
    a. "Sorry, I'm busy this afternoon."
    b. "I don't want to play with you."
	I was visiting a friend whose dog kept jumping all over my baby sister. I said,
	
	    a. "Please control your dog."
	    b. "Get your mutt out of here!"

When my friend came back to school after attending his grandmother's funeral, I said,
 	
    a. "Why weren't you in school?"
    b. "I was sorry to hear about your grandmother."
	While my friend and I were playing outside, she tripped and fell. I
	
	    a. laughed and said, "Why don't you watch where you're going?"
	    b. asked, "Are you hurt?"

_____
_____
_____
_____
 	
  a. _____
  b. _____
	_____
	_____
	_____
	_____
	
	  a. _____
	  b. _____

Section V

WOULD YOU APPLAUD YOUR AUDIENCE BEHAVIOR?

Section V makes students aware of appropriate behaviors as audience members.

Activity/Grade Level/Description

V-1 *It's My Behavior* (**K-4**) is a song for everyone to sing in the auditorium.

V-2 *Would They Want Me Back?* (**2-4**) suggests making a big book about audience etiquette prior to attending a musical or theatrical performance and evaluating student behavior afterward.

V-3 *Applauding My Audience Behavior* (**3-4**) is a booklet to be cut out and stapled by students. It is used as a ready reference and guide to appropriate audience behavior for attending a circus, movie theater, sporting event, religious service, play, concert, ballet, opera, or musical show.

V-1   IT'S MY BEHAVIOR

IT'S MY BEHAVIOR

Robert Winder, Jr.

In - to the au-di-to-ri-um I'll walk, then I'll sit down and will not talk.
thing per-for-mers gripe a-bout is watch-ing me walk in and out.

To my-self I'll keep my feet and leave them off my neigh-bor's seat.
If I need to leave the show, ve-ry quiet-ly I will go. I

When my arm I need to rest, I'll try not to be a pest. I will not bring
won't run in or out pell mell, Ne-ver, ev-er boo or yell During the performance

a-ny toys when they — they make a noise. It's my be-hav-ior
I'll be kind, and my man-ners I will mind.

— My — be-hav-ior that I ap-plaud — that I ap-plaud — It's

— that I ap-plaud. — Du —ring the show is no time to

chit, chit, chat, Nor is this the place to wear a hat! Ne-ver in-side!

D.S. al fine

you know that! some-

Section V: Would You Applaud Your Audience Behavior?

V-2   WOULD THEY WANT ME BACK?

REMEMBER THAT ON ANY FIELD TRIP, YOU REPRESENT YOUR SCHOOL, YOUR FAMILY, AND YOURSELF. YOUR BEHAVIOR TELLS OTHERS WHAT YOU THINK OF YOU!

HERE ARE SOME SUGGESTED RULES FOR POLITE BEHAVIOR:

1. WALK INTO THE THEATER IN A QUIET AND ORDERLY MANNER.

2. SIT IN YOUR SEAT WITH YOUR FEET ON THE FLOOR.

3. SPEAK QUIETLY WITH THE PERSON ON EITHER SIDE OF YOU UNTIL THE PERFORMANCE BEGINS.

4. NOW ADD RULES TO THIS LIST THAT ALLOW YOU TO HAVE AN ENJOYABLE TIME WHILE ALSO BEING POLITE TO THE PERFORMERS AND THE REST OF THE AUDIENCE.

DRAW A SCENE TO GO WITH EACH RULE:
Write the rule at the bottom of each scene. Combine the scenes in a BIG BOOK. Display the book for all to read a day or two before a field trip. After the trip, make a SELF-EVALUATION CHECKLIST.

Section V: Would You Applaud Your Audience Behavior?

APPLAUDING MY AUDIENCE BEHAVIOR

NAME _____

- Food, beverages, candy, and gum are allowed at outdoor events.
- There is some quiet talking permitted, and you may stand or walk around as long as you do not interfere with the rights of others to see and hear the music.
- If the audience is invited to participate, politely join in.
- Applaud at the end of each selection.
- Throw litter in available trash cans or take it with you when you leave.

V-3B   APPLAUDING MY AUDIENCE BEHAVIOR

- Stand for the singing of "The Star-Spangled Banner," our national anthem.

- If you bring a portable radio or small TV, use earphones to listen to it.

- Food and beverages are permitted.

- You may applaud, stand, talk, laugh, whistle, chant, sing, boo, cheer, and call out to the players in reaction to what's happening on the field or in the gymnasium, arena or stadium.

- Pick up your empty food and drink containers and throw them in a wastebasket on your way out.

- Use the restrooms and buy your refreshments *before* settling into your seat.

- Keep your hands to yourself and your feet down.

- You may laugh, cheer, boo, and cry with the audience.

- Enjoy the movie in a way that will allow others to enjoy it, too.

- Pick up your empty food and drink containers and place them in the wastebaskets on your way out.

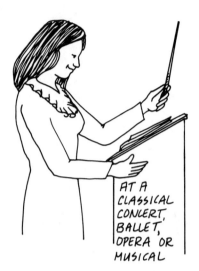

- Be in your reserved seat before the lights begin to dim.

- Stand when others in your row need to pass you to get to their seats.

- Applaud for the conductor as soon as he or she appears.

- You must be absolutely quiet as soon as the music begins.

- Applaud whenever the audience does.

- When the lights go on you may talk and leave your seat.

- Intermission is the time to use the restrooms and stand in the lobby.

- A warning bell or gong is the signal that intermission is ending and that you should return to your seat immediately.

- At the end of a performance you may shout "Brava" to a female performer, "Bravo" to a male performer, or "Bravi" to male and female performers together to show that you enjoyed them.

- If you were thrilled with the performance, you may join in a standing ovation.

- You may bring fresh flowers to throw on the stage during the applause or ask an usher to present a bouquet to a performer.

- The correct ways to show your displeasure with a performance are to leave for good at intermission or to sit quietly without applauding.

V-3D   APPLAUDING MY AUDIENCE BEHAVIOR

- Food and beverages may be brought into the circus or bought throughout the show.

- Throw empty food and drink containers in wastebaskets.

- Stay in your reserved seat except during intermission when you may stand or walk around.

- Applaud each performance during and after the act.

- It is all right to have a conversation with clowns or other performers who come into the audience.

- It is fine to talk quietly with members of your group during the circus and to point out to each other what is happening.

- Be considerate of others by not calling attention to yourself.

AT THE CIRCUS

- Upon entering, be respectful.
- You must be quiet, patient, and alert.
- Look at the behavior of the worshippers and follow their example.
- Follow the directions of the religious leader.
- Do what the adults you are with tell you to do so that you don't embarrass yourself.

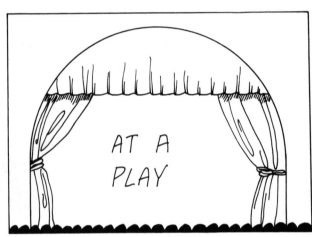

- You may talk quietly in your seat before the lights dim.
- Stand for people coming into your row.
- Stay in your reserved or assigned seat.
- Sit still so that the person behind you can see.
- Show your appreciation for the performers by applauding or laughing when the audience does.
- Keep your feet and hands to yourself.
- Wait until intermission to leave your seat.
- During intermission use the restroom and stand in the lobby or aisle.
- Be alert to the end of intermission and return to your seat on time.
- Applaud during curtain calls. If you thought the performance was really outstanding, you may join the audience in a standing ovation.

Section VI

WOULD YOU WIN VOTES FOR VISITING?

This section is designed to cultivate civility while on field or family trips to private and public places.

Activity/Grade Level/Description

VI-1   *Hurray, Here We Go* (K-4) is a song that reinforces the rules of good bus behavior. It is sung to the tune of "Ninety-nine Bottles of Beer on the Wall."

VI-2   *Zing a Zoo Zong* (K-2) is a song that highlights desirable behaviors while on a trip to the zoo. Your class might try to add verses or to vary the rhymes for a different trip. It is sung to the tune of "Old MacDonald."

VI-3   *Come On Over* (1-2) is a whole-class activity guided by the teacher. The host exhibits appropriate behavior; the guest, on the other hand, is rude throughout the visit. Divide the class into hosts and guests. Each group will evaluate the comments on its side of the gameboard, moving alphabetically. Encourage discussion and alternative language, especially where rude behavior is evident, before moving to the next box.

VI-4   *Courteous Correspondence* (1-4) provides a sample invitation and thank-you note followed by forms for practice. It teaches students to write clear and concise invitations, encourages them to respond to invitations, and to show appreciation for hospitality by means of thank-you letters.

VI-5   *Destination U.S.A.* (3-4) is an exciting and enjoyable board game that takes students on a well-mannered tour of historical, cultural, and natural sites throughout the United States. Along the route, progress and setbacks are determined by chance as each player takes a card. Acceptable ways of behaving in public places are taught.

Go over the following directions with the students to make sure they understand how to play:

1. Shuffle the cards and place them face down on the gameboard.
2. Decide who goes first using a die, spinner, etc.
3. Begin the game by taking a card from the top of the pile. Read and follow the directions on the card.
4. If you get an ENTRANCE card, save it until you need it. After using the ENTRANCE card, place it somewhere in the middle of the pile of cards on the gameboard. If a card tells you to **Leave the Game,** the ENTRANCE card will get you back in the game, but you must begin at Start.
5. The winner is the first player to complete the trip.

VI-I   HURRAY, HERE WE GO

We're off on a bus trip,
Hurray, here we go;
We're off to the _____

_____.

Before we pull out
Here are rules we must know,
Then safe and secure we
  will be to and fro.

The first thing we do is
  sit down in a seat;
Sit and remain there for good.
A lurch or a stop and the
  windshield we'd greet,
Listen 'cause this good
  advice can't be beat.

Our teachers will open the
  windows for air,
We will not touch them ourselves.
We won't put our heads,
  hands, nose, toes, feet out there,
Nor will we litter. We'll show
  that we care.

We don't need to scream,
  yell or shout to be heard.
Pity the bus driver's ears.
Hat grabbing, skin pinching
  uncool and absurd,
Quietly talking, yes, that's
  the last word.

If gum you are chewing
  keep it off the floor,
And off your friend and
  your seat.
Pick up all your litter
  and anything more.
Wait for directions
  to go out the door.

Chorus: Here come the children to the zoo
    Oh wow, oh wow, oh wow.
The animals are watching you.
    Oh wow, oh wow, oh wow.

Verse #1: Lost buddy here, no buddy there,
Here a buddy, there a buddy,
Everybody needs a buddy.

The animals are watching you
    Oh wow, oh wow, oh wow.
Repeat Chorus

Verse #2: Litter here, litter there,
Here a trash can, there a trash can,
Litter goes inside the trash can.
Lost buddy here, no buddy there,
Here a buddy, there a buddy,
Everybody needs a buddy.

The animals are watching you
    Oh wow, oh wow, oh wow.
Repeat Chorus

Verse #3: No running here, no running there,
Here you walk, there you walk,
Everyone walks everywhere.
Litter here, litter there,
Here a trash can, there a trash can.
Lost buddy here, no buddy there,
Here a buddy, there a buddy,
Everybody needs a buddy.

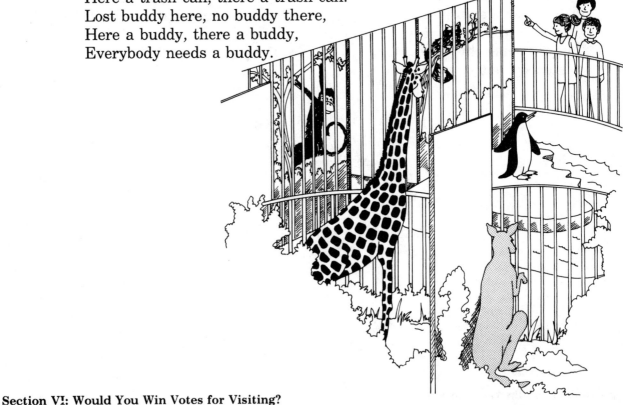

VI-2B ZING A ZOO ZONG

The animals are watching you
Oh wow, oh wow, oh wow.
Repeat Chorus

Verse #4:   No feeding here, no feeding there,
Feed yourself, not the bear,
"Do Not Feed" signs everywhere.
No running here, no running there,
Here you walk, there you walk,
Everyone walks everywhere.
Litter here, litter there,
Here a trash can, there a trash can,
Litter goes inside the trash can.
Lost buddy here, no buddy there,
Here a buddy, there a buddy,
Everybody needs a buddy.

The animals are watching you
  Oh wow, oh wow, oh wow.
Repeat Chorus

Verse #5:   Tap a case here, make a face there,
You bother us, don't bother us,
It's time to get back on the bus.
No feeding here, no feeding there,
Feed yourself, not the bear,
"Do Not Feed" signs everywhere.
No running here, no running there,
Here you walk, there you walk,
Everyone walks everywhere.
Litter here, litter there,
Here a trash can, there a trash can,
Litter goes inside the trash can.
Lost buddy here, no buddy there,
Here a buddy, there a buddy,
Everybody needs a buddy.

The animals are watching you
  Oh wow, oh wow, oh wow.

VI-3 COME ON OVER!

Section VI: Would You Win Votes for Visiting?

VI-4A   COURTEOUS CORRESPONDENCE

YOU'RE INVITED

TO: A birthday party

FOR: Perry Penguin

AT: 12 Igloo Drive, Nome, Alaska

DATE: January 5

TIME: 2:00 P.M. to 4:00 P.M.

R.S.V.P. by January 1   1-907-234-5678

WHEN YOU RECEIVE AN INVITATION, IT IS IMPORTANT THAT YOU R.S.V.P, WHICH IS FRENCH FOR "RESPOND PLEASE!"

YOU'RE INVITED

TO: _____

FOR: _____

AT: _____

DATE: _____

TIME: _____

R.S.V.P. _____

MAKE SURE TO INCLUDE WHO, WHAT, WHEN, WHERE, AND WHY WHEN SENDING AN INVITATION.

Section VI: Would You Win Votes for Visiting?

Name _____ Date _____

VI-4B COURTEOUS CORRESPONDENCE

> August 15
>
> Dear Gerry,
>   Thank you for the wonderful week I spent at your house. I had fun playing with you and visiting Waterloo Village and going to the movies. The Empire State Building was awesome.
>   I hope you can visit me next summer.
>
> Love,
>
> Chee Chee

WHEN FRIENDS AND RELATIVES SPEND TIME AND MONEY TO ENTERTAIN YOU, IT IS THOUGHTFUL TO EXPRESS YOUR APPRECIATION IN A THANK YOU NOTE.

IT'S NICE TO KNOW THAT MY HOSPITALITY WAS ENJOYED AND APPECIATED.

Dear _____,

_____

_____

_____

_____

_____

Love,

_____

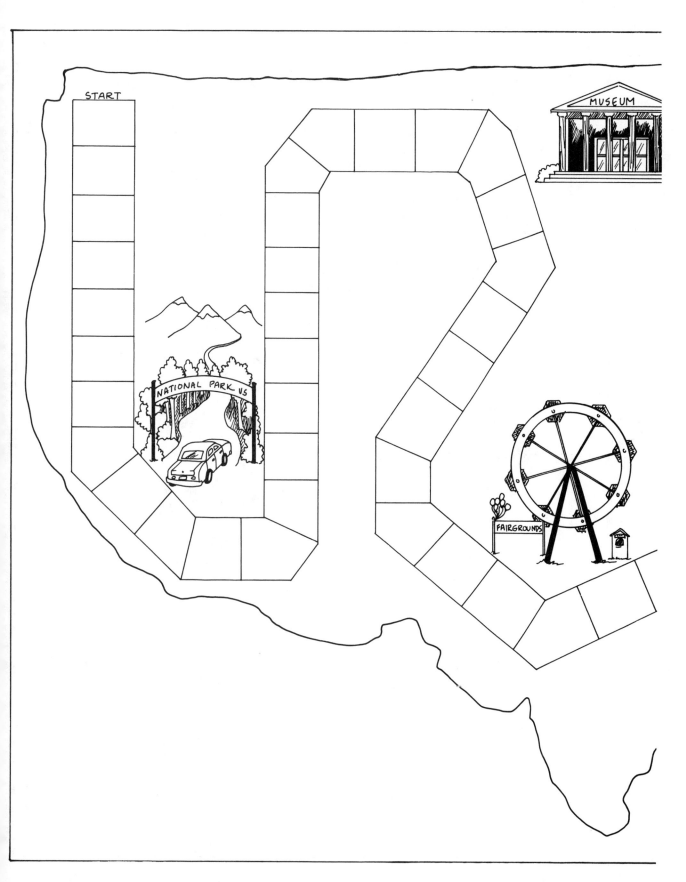

Section VI: Would You Win Votes for Visiting?

VI-5B DESTINATION U.S.A.

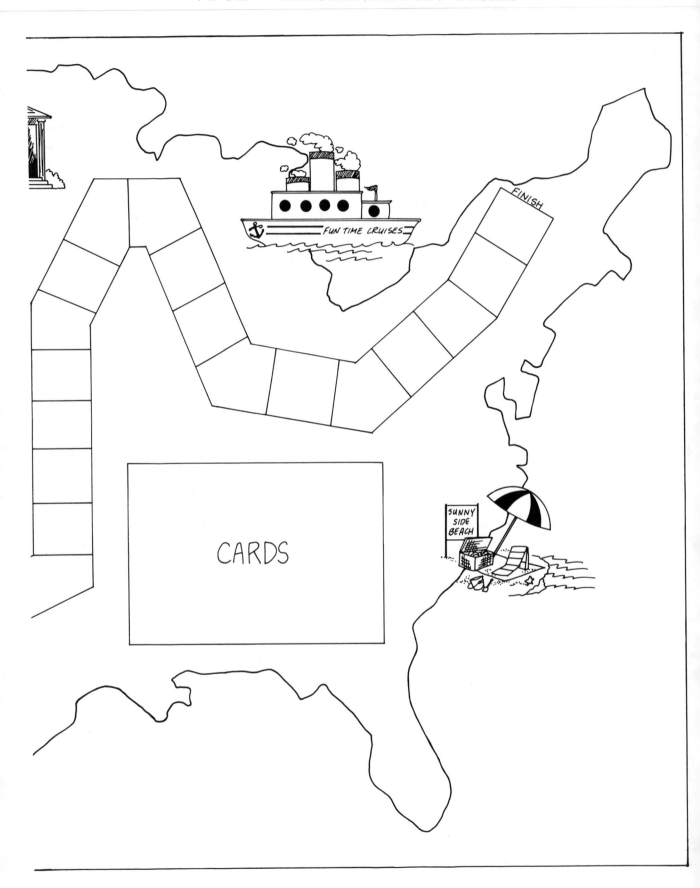

Section VI: Would You Win Votes for Visiting?

While touring Wind Cave Limestone Caverns in South Dakota, you kept your hands off the stalagtites and stalagmites. **Move ahead one space.**	At an Olympic National Park campsite in Washington, you kept the volume of your portable radio low so as not to disturb other campers. **Move ahead three spaces.**
At Walt Disney World in Florida you waited patiently on a long line to visit Epcot Center. **Pick another card.**	During a religious service at the National Cathedral in Washington, D.C., you were quiet and stood or sat when others did. **Take two turns.**
While attending the Sugar Bowl in Louisiana, you politely asked the person in front of you to sit down. **Move ahead one space.**	While walking along the Snake River Trail in Idaho, you stopped to allow faster hikers to pass you. **Move ahead one space.**
At Isle Royale, Michigan, you stood very quietly and still to observe a moose. **Go ahead two spaces.**	While in the Metropolitan Museum of Art in New York, you walked and talked quietly as your group looked at the art work. **Move ahead two spaces.**
While on a cruise ship in Alaska, you allowed shorter children to stand in front of you so they could see the icebergs. **Move ahead one space.**	After a picnic at Waterloo Village in New Jersey, you threw your litter in the garbage can. **Move ahead three spaces.**

Section VI: Would You Win Votes for Visiting?

While visiting a school in Tulsa, Oklahoma, you walked quietly into the building and through the halls. **Move ahead one space.**	At Yellowstone National Park in Wyoming, you remained with the group on the paths and boardwalks. **Move ahead three spaces.**
While following the guide through the Governor's Mansion in Williamsburg, Virginia, you kept a safe distance from the antiques. **Pick another card.**	As you entered the State House in Santa Fe, New Mexico, you removed your hat. **Move ahead one space.**
At the zoo in Chicago, Illinois, you looked at, but did not annoy or feed the animals. **Move ahead one space.**	Along the Ridge Trail in the Rocky Mountains of Colorado, you were careful not to harm any of the plant life on the tundra. **Take two turns.**
You walked, not ran in the pool area at your condominium at Hilton Head, South Carolina. **Move ahead one space.**	While visiting another classroom in your school, you kept your hands out of the students' desks. **Move ahead two spaces.**

VI-5E   DESTINATION U.S.A.

While at a backyard party at a friend's house in Atlanta, Georgia, you shook a can of soda and it squirted on everyone around you. **Lose two turns.**	At Big Bone Lick in Kentucky, you tried to take a fossil of a mammoth. The guide stopped you. **Go back three spaces and miss a turn.**
At the Pueblo ruins in Arizona, you broke off a piece of the Indian house and put it in your pocket. **Leave the game.**	While purchasing a fishing license in the Bangor, Maine Town Hall, you left your family to wander through the offices. **Move back one space.**
You opened a door that said NOT OPEN TO THE PUBLIC in Laura Ingalls Wilder's house in Missouri. **Go back one space.**	At the Whitney Museum in New York, you touched a painting and the alarm went off. **Lose two turns.**
While at Longwood Gardens in Delaware, you picked a flower. **Return to Start.**	At one of the Newport, Rhode Island "cottages," you stooped under a velvet rope to play the antique piano. **Go back three spaces.**

ENTRANCE	You're really showing consideration for others. **Move ahead six spaces.**
Congratulations. Your manners are great! **Move ahead five spaces.**	While attending a friend's Bar Mitzvah, you talked loudly and giggled during the religious service at the synagogue in Cleveland, Ohio. **Move back three spaces.**
ENTRANCE	You wore shorts to the Mormon Temple in Salt Lake City, Utah and were not admitted. **Lose your turn.**
Terrific behavior! **Move ahead four spaces.**	While visiting an Amish farm in Lancaster, Pennsylvania, you teased an 800-pound bull and it ran towards the fence at you. **Move back two spaces.**

VI-5G   DESTINATION U.S.A.

While driving through Iron Mountain, Wisconsin, you threw garbage out the car window. **If you have an ENTRANCE card, give it to the person on your left. If not, lose two turns.**	At Lake Winnibigoshish, Minnesota, you took a hotdog to the swimming area and were told to leave. **Move back one space.**
After a clambake at Myrtle Beach, North Carolina, you didn't clean up the area and left the fire glowing. **Return to Start.**	While visiting your cousin's classroom in Mobile, Alabama, you pulled something off the bulletin board. **Lose a turn.**
You jumped off the side of the hotel pool in Wichita, Kansas, nearly hitting and hurting someone. **Go back three spaces.**	At the Sturbridge Village gift shop in Massachusetts, you stole a postcard. **Leave the game.**
You visited the Alamo in Texas and wrote your initials on the wall of the fort. **Return to Start.**	You really are obnoxious. **Go back five spaces.**

Your behavior is unacceptable. **Go back four spaces.**	
You have embarrassed yourself and annoyed everyone. **Go back six spaces.**	

Section VII

DO YOUR TABLE MANNERS MAKE IT?

The activities in this section lead students through progressively demanding rules of table etiquette at meals in different settings.

Activity/Grade Level/Description

VII-1 *What a Mess!* **(K)** earns its title from the amusing illustration of a child who has made a mess of his meal. Students will talk about the picture and about how to stay neat at the table.

VII-2 *I Remembered!* **(K)** is a pictorial reminder to use one's napkin.

VII-3 *Gee Mom, You're Good* **(1)** is a matching game similar to Bingo. All students get the full sheet with Mother Raccoon. The Young Raccoon sheet should be cut apart into 16 tokens. Explain the directions on page VII-3A; then read the activities out of sequence.

VII-4 *Raccoon Wreck!* **(1)** is a fun activity that confirms the right and wrong ways to behave at a meal.

VII-5 *Igloo Etiquette* **(2)** illustrates the table manners expected of second graders. Students talk about the good table manners they see.

VII-6 *Dining Hall Disaster* **(3)** is meant to amuse and shock students with the disgraceful antics of the chimps at camp. Students are asked to write a story about how they would feel at this camp lunch. After hearing the stories read aloud, a discussion of proper table behavior in a casual setting can take place.

VII-7 *My Birthday Party* **(3)** is a question-and-answer activity that compares appropriate and inappropriate behavior in a fast-food restaurant. Follow the activity with a discussion.

VII-8 *Posh Nosh* **(4)** is an entertaining board game that teaches and reinforces the *best* table manners. It asks students to draw conclusions about expectations of etiquette at an elegant and expensive restaurant. At the end of the game, students are invited to a dinner at the White House. After taking the quiz, everyone with a score of 80 percent or more earns an "Outstanding Table Manners Award."

VII-1   WHAT A MESS!

Let's talk about this picture. Can you use color to show how very sloppy Sam is?

Section VII: Do Your Table Manners Make It?

VII-2   I REMEMBERED!

VII-3A   GEE MOM, YOU'RE GOOD

DIRECTIONS TO THE TEACHER

This is a matching game much like BINGO except everyone who plays can win at the same time by:

    a. listening to and understanding oral directions

    b. recognizing and selecting illustrations that mirror those on the gameboard

    c. placing and completing each lettered square

Players need pages VII-3B and VII-3C. VII-3B will be used as a gameboard, while the illustrations on page VII-3C will be used as tokens during the game to complete gameboard pictures.

In order for the game to provide positive reinforcement and maintain high interest, it is suggested that the order of the actions below be read aloud out of sequence.

After a student or group has won, continue the game until every picture has been matched. Discuss all the actions in sequence.

_____ A. Randy helps Mother set the table.

_____ B. Randy sits at the table.

_____ C. Randy picks up the napkin.

_____ D. The open napkin is placed on Randy's lap.

_____ E. Randy picks up the knife and fork.

_____ F. Randy sticks the fork into the meat with his/her right hand.

_____ G. Randy rests the knife on the edge of his/her plate.

_____ H. Randy raises the meat on the fork to his/her mouth.

_____ I. With mouth closed, Randy chews the meat.

_____ J. Randy swallows all the chewed meat.

_____ K. After placing the fork on the plate, Randy picks up the drink.

_____ L. Randy sips—not gulps—the drink.

_____ M. Randy sets the glass, carefully, back on the table.

_____ N. Randy wipes his/her mouth with the napkin.

_____ O. Randy puts the napkin back on the table.

_____ P. Randy accidently knocks the glass over. OOPS!

Section VII: Do Your Table Manners Make It?

Section VII: Do Your Table Manners Make It?

VII-4   RACCOON WRECK!

PLEASE FIND AND CIRCLE TEN THINGS THAT I WOULD <u>NEVER</u> DO.

Section VII: Do Your Table Manners Make It?

VII-5   IGLOO ETIQUETTE

Section VII: Do Your Table Manners Make It?

Pretend you are Chee Chee Chimp.
Write a story about your thoughts
and feelings at this lunch.

CHEE CHEE

WHAT A DISASTER!

CAMP RUN-A-MUCK

I CAN'T BELIEVE THEY DROPPED ALL THIS FOOD ON THE FLOOR.

WE'LL BE EATING THIS MESS FOR A WEEK.

WORMS

Section VII: Do Your Table Manners Make It?

Section VII: Do Your Table Manners Make It?

Name _____ **Date** _____

VII-7B   MY BIRTHDAY PARTY

Answer these questions:

1. I'd be sorry I'd invited these kids to my party because _____

_____

_____

_____

_____

2. I'd be glad I'd invited these friends because _____

_____

_____

_____

_____

Discuss with your classmates:

1. What does each illustration show?

2. What do you feel about each illustration?

3. What were your reasons for feeling sorry or glad?

4. How could poor table manners ruin your party?

5. How would you plan differently for your next party?

Name _____ Date _____

VII-8A   POSH NOSH

PLAY A GAME AT "POSH NOSH," AN ELEGANT AND EXPENSIVE PLACE TO DINE. WILL YOU FEEL CONFIDENT AND PROUD? OR WILL THE WAITER HAVE TO ASK YOU TO LEAVE?

For 3, 4, or 5 players:

—Use a spinner or die to determine the order of players.

—The player with the highest number starts.

—All players place their markers (colored paper squares, buttons, etc.) at the entrance to Posh Nosh, an elegant and expensive restaurant.

—Each player uses the spinner or die to find out how many spaces to move. He/she reads aloud the situation with its reward or consequence. If sent away from the table, lose one turn.

—At the end of the game, the exact number needed must be spun in order to land on square #16.

—All players play through the entire game.

VII-8B   POSH NOSH

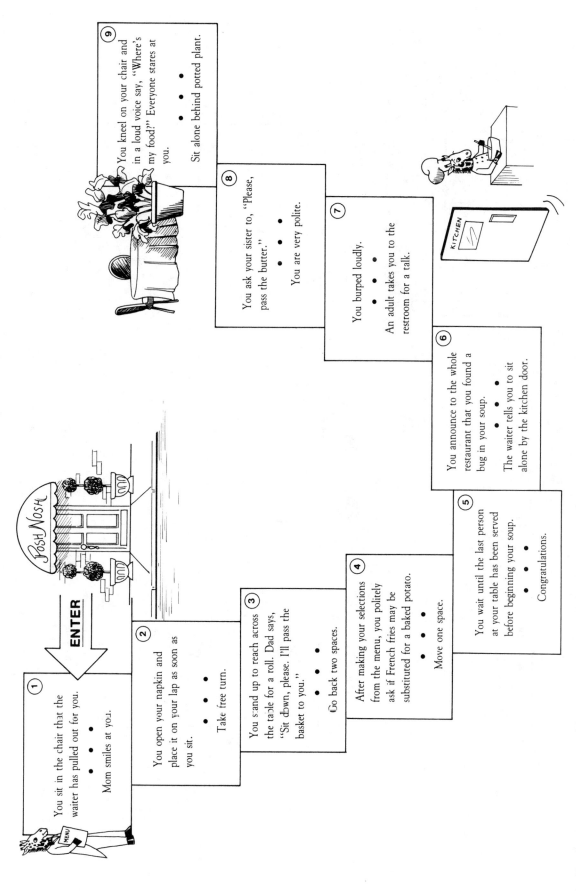

ENTER

1. You sit in the chair that the waiter has pulled out for you.
   - Mom smiles at you.

2. You open your napkin and place it on your lap as soon as you sit.
   - Take free turn.

3. You stand up to reach across the table for a roll. Dad says, "Sit down, please. I'll pass the basket to you."
   - Go back two spaces.

4. After making your selections from the menu, you politely ask if French fries may be substituted for a baked potato.
   - Move one space.

5. You wait until the last person at your table has been served before beginning your soup.
   - Congratulations.

6. You announce to the whole restaurant that you found a bug in your soup.
   - The waiter tells you to sit alone by the kitchen door.

7. You burped loudly.
   - An adult takes you to the restroom for a talk.

8. You ask your sister to, "Please, pass the butter."
   - You are very polite.

9. You kneel on your chair and in a loud voice say, "Where's my food?" Everyone stares at you.
   - Sit alone behind potted plant.

Section VII: Do Your Table Manners Make It?

VII-8C POSH NOSH (continued)

10

The waiter brings your entrée and you say, "Thank You."

-
-

Take free turn.

11

A pea from your sister's plate flies across the table. You throw it back at her.

-

Wait in the car until you lose one turn. Then begin at start.

12

You use your fingernail to remove food that's stuck between your teeth.

-

Go back three spaces.

13

After dropping your fork you motion to the waiter to bring you another.

-

You receive the Blue Ribbon Award.

14

You ask the waiter for ketchup for your Veau Veronique. (That's French for veal with grapes.)

-
-

Move back one space.

15

While talking with your mouth full, some ice cream drips onto the tablecloth.

-

Go back to #8.

16

Your invitation to a State Dinner at the White House is hand delivered to you by your teacher.

State aloud one thing you learned while playing this game before getting your invitation.

-
-

Blue Ribbon Dining.

Section VII: Do Your Table Manners Make It?

Your polite presence
is requested
at
The White House
for a
formal state dinner.

VII-8E   POSH NOSH

1. When dressing to go to a fancy restaurant, you wear _____
   a. blue jeans, sneakers, and a T-shirt.
   b. a dress or a suit or other dress-up clothes.
   c. shorts, a tank top, and thongs.
2. When the waiter pulls out a chair for you, you _____
   a. pull out a different one for yourself.
   b. say, "Thank you" and sit down.
   c. say, "Are you planning to eat with us?"
3. As soon as you sit, you _____
   a. open your napkin and place it on your lap.
   b. say, "I have to go to the bathroom."
   c. point to someone across the room and yell, "Look at that fat lady!"
4. When the rolls and butter are brought to the table, you _____
   a. grab one before the basket hits the table.
   b. reach quickly across the table, knocking over a glass of water.
   c. say, "Please pass the rolls and butter."
5. When the waiter comes to take your order, you _____
   a. say, "I hate everything on this menu."
   b. ask, "Where does it say hot dogs and hamburgers?"
   c. ask, "Would it be possible to substitute corn for the broccoli?"
6. When the soup arrives, you _____
   a. slurp it.
   b. wait until everyone at the table has been served before picking up your spoon.
   c. lift up the soup bowl and drink from it.
7. After noticing a hair in your salad, you _____
   a. announce it to the whole restaurant.
   b. quietly motion to the waiter to look, then remove the plate.
   c. hold up the hair and say, "Eeeeuw!"
8. When a piece of corn gets stuck between your teeth, you _____
   a. excuse yourself from the table to go to the bathroom to remove it.
   b. ask the waiter for a toothpick.
   c. dig it out with your fingernail.
9. With your mouth full of food, you _____
   a. chew, swallow, then start to speak.
   b. start talking.
   c. take a drink.
10. When the check is brought to the table, you _____
    a. grab it to see how much the meal cost.
    b. ask the adult who is reading it how much the meal cost.
    c. ignore the check and, after you have left the restaurant, ask how much the meal cost. (Don't expect an answer.)

SCORE: _____ (You must earn a score of 80% or more in order to receive "The Outstanding Table Manners Award.")

Section VII: Do Your Table Manners Make It?

Section VIII

ARE YOUR LOOKS LIKEABLE?

Section VIII guides students to become aware that facial expressions, body language, hygiene/grooming, and attire communicate who they are and what they feel. Appropriate choices build esteem and confidence.

Activity/Grade Level/Description

VIII-1   *I Know! I Know!* **(K-4)** is a checklist for students to complete at home. The activity encourages them to develop good habits of grooming and hygiene. Those who return the completed chart receive "A Pat on the Back."

VIII-2   *What Is Your Face Saying?* **(K-4)** is a collection of facial expressions that students are asked to interpret for the inner feelings they might reveal. Students are made aware that their facial expressions can cause a variety of responses from other people. While proceeding through the steps in this activity, students will realize that facial expressions can invite or discourage positive reactions from other people.

       In this activity, we suggest the integration of language arts (adjectives, vocabulary development, thesaurus use, spelling), thinking skills (analysis, synthesis), and emotional health. All of these can be addressed through a bulletin board display, mobiles, collages, and role playing.

VIII-3   *Where to Wear?* **(K-2)** is a card game similar to "Go Fish." Students sharpen their observation and classification skills while choosing appropriate clothing for eight different occasions. Make four copies of sheets VIII-3B through VIII-3E and cut apart the cards. Sheet VIII-3F is blank so that the children can draw their own illustrations of clothes for the various occasions.

       Note the symbols on the game cards and their meanings: *religious service*—a cross, Star of David, and crescent; *wedding*—a bouquet of flowers; *picnic*—a hotdog; *school*—an apple; *zoo*—an elephant's head; *opera*—musical notes; *museum*—a painting; *holiday party*—a party hat and favors.

VIII-4   ***Don't Embarrass Yourself!*** **(3-4)** suggests appropriate attire for three dissimilar occasions. "Would you wear sneakers to a wedding, a bathing suit to school, or a fancy dress/suit to a Fourth of July parade?" These are some humorous questions students can answer prior to beginning the activity.

VIII-5   ***Slouch Grouch*** **(3-4)** is a multi-faceted activity that incorporates role playing, dialogue writing, oral presenting, observing, analyzing, synthesizing, and discussing. The goal is the realization that body language—facial expressions and movements of the body and the methods of combining them to be used and understood by a considerable community—is another form of communication.

Name _____ Date _____

VIII-1A I KNOW! I KNOW!

HERE'S A CHECKLIST TO TAKE HOME MONDAY NIGHT. PUT AN X IN EACH BOX AS YOU COMPLETE EVERY GROOMING ACTIVITY. RETURN THIS PAPER FRIDAY WITH A GROWN-UP'S SIGNATURE AT THE BOTTOM. CAN YOU DO THESE THINGS WITHOUT BEING TOLD?

I'm Making My Looks Likeable By:	Tuesday A.M.	Tuesday P.M.	Wednesday A.M.	Wednesday P.M.	Thursday A.M.	Thursday P.M.
Brushing My Teeth						
Washing My Face						
Fixing My Hair						
Washing My Hands After Going to the Bathroom						
Washing My Hands Before Eating						
Wearing Freshly Washed Underwear and Socks						
Choosing Clothes with Colors That Go Together						
Taking a Bath or a Shower						
Washing My Hair						
Using Tissues to Blow My Nose or to Cover My Mouth When I Cough						

_____ completed this chart honestly. He/she deserves a pat on the
Student's Name   back

for likeable looks.

_____
Parent or Guardian Signature

Section VIII: Are Your Looks Likeable?

VIII-2A   WHAT IS YOUR FACE SAYING?

DIRECTIONS FOR THE TEACHER

1. Distribute copies of the activity.
2. Have the class discuss what they see in the faces and answer the questions together.
3. As students name feelings, such as happy, ask "What would make a person feel happy?" Elicit different situations that created the feeling and have the students suggest vocabulary even more specific to the situation. See the Vocabulary List for help.
4. Have students look through magazines, either as a class activity or for homework, to find large, expressive faces and cut them out. Put the faces on display. Have students suggest and list the feelings expressed on these faces.
5. Now answer and discuss these questions: "With whom would you want to spend time? How can you help yourself get over negative feelings that everyone has from time to time?"

Vocabulary List of Feelings

Happy	nice, pleasing, attractive, agreeable, appealing, genteel, ecstatic, glad, felicitous, blissful, overjoyed, surprised
Kind	gentle, sympathetic, tender, friendly, solicitous, helpful, sensitive, warm
Funny	mischievous, elfish, impish, amused, silly
Angry	sullen, resentful, ill-tempered, sour, surly, morose, glum, moody, sulky, pouting, grumpy, peevish, bored, depressed (anger turned inward), annoyed, disgusted
Sad	unhappy, sorrowful, downcast, dejected, woeful, gloomy, melancholy, disappointed, miserable, wretched, forlorn, doleful, pained
Lively	enthusiastic, vivacious, excited, delighted, eager
Hateful	mean, hostile, bitter, spiteful, malicious, obnoxious, disagreeable, repulsive, cold
Stubborn	inflexible, willful
Bragging	arrogant, haughty, overbearing
Complaining	nagging, criticizing, accusing, mocking
Afraid	fearful, scared, insecure
Serious	earnest, intent, solemn, determined, purposeful, conscientious
Doubting	incredulous, unbelieving, distrusting, suspicious, shocked
Tired	sleepy, fatigued, weary, exhausted, listless
Uninterested	indifferent, unconcerned, devil-may-care, blasé, dull, unambitious, apathetic
Curious	inquisitive, questioning, prying, meddlesome
Easygoing	yielding, soft, docile, submissive, compliant

VIII-2B   WHAT IS YOUR FACE SAYING?

LOOK AT EACH FACE. FEELINGS ARE OFTEN SHOWN ON OUR FACES. WHAT MIGHT THESE FACES BE EXPRESSING AND WHY?

Name _____ Date _____

VIII-3A   WHERE TO WEAR?

WHAT YOU WEAR TELLS OTHERS HOW YOU FEEL ABOUT YOURSELF AND THEM!

CUT OUT THE CARDS WITH THE DIFFERENT ITEMS OF CLOTHING ON THEM. PLACE THE SHUFFLED CARDS FACE DOWN IN A PILE BETWEEN THE PLAYERS. DECIDE WHO WILL GO FIRST AND DEAL.

THE GAME CAN BE PLAYED WITH 2 OR 3 PLAYERS. EACH PLAYER GETS 3 CARDS FACE DOWN. CAREFULLY LOOK AT YOUR CARDS. WHEN IT IS YOUR TURN, ASK THE PERSON ON YOUR LEFT FOR A CARD WHICH WILL HELP TO COMPLETE ONE OF THE EVENT CARDS IN YOUR HAND.

EXAMPLE: "DO YOU HAVE A WEDDING CARD (SYMBOL)?" IF THE PLAYER SAYS, "NO", THEN YOU WILL GO SHOPPING BY TAKING THE TOP CARD FROM THE DECK. THE OBJECT OF THE GAME IS TO HAVE THE MOST SETS OF 4 CARDS WITH THE SAME SYMBOLS.

VIII-3C   WHERE TO WEAR?

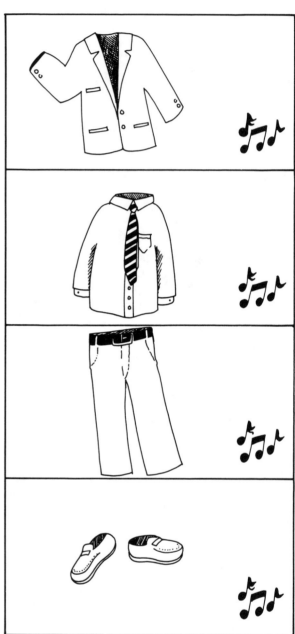

VIII-3E   WHERE TO WEAR?

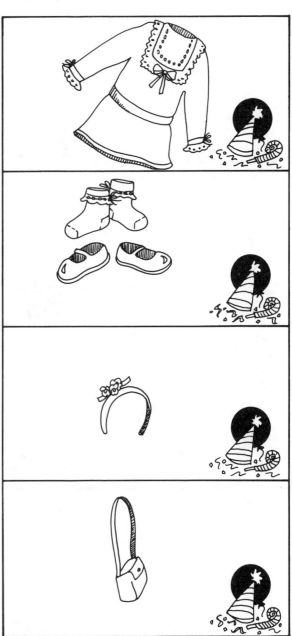

VIII-3F   WHERE TO WEAR?

Name _____ Date _____

VIII-4A   DON'T EMBARRASS YOURSELF!

VIII-5A   SLOUCH GROUCH

DIRECTIONS FOR THE TEACHER

1. In an effort to illustrate how body language communicates our thoughts and feelings, act out the following scene with a student:

   A student feels the teacher doesn't care about him/her and slouches constantly to show anger and disrespect. What dialogue can take place between them and how can they resolve their conflict?

2. Lead the discussion after the presentation to ensure that body language has been defined and observed (you may wish to do this first). Distribute the Body Language and Facial Expressions list.

3. Present the dialogue model either on the board or overhead projector as an introduction to writing their own dialogues about body language expressions of conflict.

4. Pair students and give them the Dialogue Form. At this time elicit suggestions for place, time, and role (i.e., two students, mother–daughter, father–son, brother–sister, etc.).

5. After students complete their dialogues, have them act out their script. (All students will have an Observation Form to complete while watching the performances.)

6. After each performance, discuss what was observed and what the body language/facial expressions might have meant. Follow by eliciting positive alternatives.

7. After the completion of all skits, list additional examples of positive body language and facial expressions that did not come out in the previous discussions (i.e., hand wave, pat on the back, etc.).

VIII-5B   SLOUCH GROUCH

Partial List of Body Language
and Facial Expressions

No eye contact
Slouching
Tapping feet
Muttering
Feet on chair or desk
Pursing lips
Smirking
Scowling

Stamping feet
Arms folded
Back turned
Mouthing words
Elbows on table or desk resting
Eyes rolling
Frowning
Fingers drumming

_____

_____

_____

_____

_____

_____

_____

_____

_____

_____

_____

_____

_____

_____

_____

_____

_____

_____

_____

Sample Dialogue Form

CHARACTER 1: <u>TEACHER</u>   (With frown on face, leaning toward the student, yells) Sit up, Clyde. I'm tired of seeing you slouch.

_____

_____

CHARACTER 2: <u>CLYDE</u>   (Slowly sits up with eyes rolling and a look of disgust on his face as he mouths silently the word "I don't care." He then proceeds to slouch again.)

_____

_____

CHARACTER 1: _____

_____

_____

CHARACTER 2: _____

_____

_____

Name _____ **Date** _____

VIII-5D   SLOUCH GROUCH

REMEMBER WHEN YOU DID SOMETHING JUST TO GET ATTENTION? THERE ARE TWO KINDS OF ATTENTION — POSITIVE AND NEGATIVE.

THE DIALOGUE FORM BELOW WILL HELP YOU WRITE A DIALOGUE BETWEEN TWO CHARACTERS, ONE OF WHOM USES AS MUCH NEGATIVE BODY LANGUAGE AS POSSIBLE.

Dialogue Form

CHARACTER 1: _____

_____

_____

_____

CHARACTER 2: _____

_____

_____

_____

CHARACTER 1: _____

_____

_____

_____

CHARACTER 2: _____

_____

_____

_____

VIII-5E   SLOUCH GROUCH

Observation Form

I observed the following body language in _____

and _____ dialogue _____

_____

_____

_____

_____

I observed the following body language in _____

and _____ dialogue _____

_____

_____

_____

_____

I observed the following body language in _____

and _____ dialogue _____

_____

_____

_____

_____

I observed the following body language in _____

and _____ dialogue _____

_____

_____

_____

_____

APPENDIX

GLOSSARY

A

absurd   ridiculously unreasonable; unsound

abundant   existing in great supply; very plentiful

adjective   a word that describes a person, place, or thing

affable   easy to talk to or approach; polite, friendly

androgynous   having both male and female characteristics

anecdote   a short story about something interesting that has happened

applaud   to express enjoyment or approval especially by clapping the hands

appreciation   a feeling of being thankful; gratitude

appropriate   suitable; proper

arena   the central part of an amphitheater or similar place used for entertainment

atrocious   very bad

audience   the people gathered to see or hear something such as a play, movie, concert or game

authority   a person appealed to as an expert; a person having certain powers

B

behavior   the way someone shows good or bad manners in front of others

body language   communication by means of gestures and/or facial expressions

bossy   inclined to act like a boss; domineering

braille   a system of writing and printing for the blind in which the letters are represented by raised dots in patterns that may be recognized and read by touching them. From Louis Braille, 1809–1852, a blind French teacher of the blind who developed this system.

bravo   Well done! Good!

C

chant a melody with many words sung on the same note. A calling or shouting of words.

characteristic special quality or feature

confide to show confidence by telling secrets; to tell in confidence; entrust

confident certain, sure, firmly believing

considerate thoughtful of the rights and feelings of others

correspond to communicate by exchanging letters

courteous marked by respect for and consideration for others

critique a critical estimate of an oral presentation

D

decent according to accepted standards; proper; kind, thoughtful

decipher to translate by using a key

decode to change from code into the original language

destination a place to which a person is going

dialogue a conversation between two or more persons; the parts that are conversation in a play or story

disaster an event that causes a "big mess"

disturb to throw into disorder; make uneasy; to inconvenience

diversity unlikeness; variation

E

elderly approaching old age

elegant rich and fine in quality

embarrass to confuse; upset

entree the main course at dinner

ethnicity national classification or affiliation

etiquette rules that tell people how to behave in various social situations

expression (facial) a facial aspect or look that indicates a certain mood or feeling

F

friendship   friendly attachment between persons

G

gender   pertaining to male or female

gross   very wrong; vulgar

group   three or more persons found together or thought of as forming a unit

H

hospitality   generous and kindly reception and entertainment of visitors and guests

I

inappropriate   not appropriate; unsuitable

interaction   action on each other

introduction   the act of introducing or state of being introduced

L

likeable   pleasing, agreeable

looks   outward appearance

M

manners   social conduct or rules of conduct; behavior

mimic   to imitate the speech, manners, or gestures of, especially so as to make fun of

N

nosh   a snack

O

obnoxious extremely disagreeable

occasion an event or function thought of as being special or important

ovation enthusiastic applause

P

patience the ability to wait a long time without complaining

politely marked by courtesy, good breeding or tact

posh elegant

prejudice opinion formed without taking time and care to judge fairly

proper strictly following rules or conventions, especially in social behavior

property something (as land, goods or money) that is owned

proud pleased at having done something well

public relating to or affecting all people

Q

quality something special about a person or object that makes it what it is

S

sarcastic using words that normally mean one thing to mean just the opposite, usually to hurt someone's feelings or to show scorn

secure literally "free from care"; easy in mind

sloppy very untidy, messy

slur an insult

society human beings as a group; a group of people forming a community and having common interests, traditions and cultures

sportsmanship fair play or ability to accept defeat graciously

symbol something that stands for or represents something else

T

tactful having or showing a keen understanding of how to get along with other people

tactic   procedure to gain advantage or success; method

talent   a natural ability or skill

taunt   to mock or reproach with insults or scornful language

tease   to annoy or make fun of playfully or mischievously

thesaurus   a dictionary of synonyms (words that mean the same or almost the same)

thoughtful   careful of others; considerate; giving careful attention to the comfort or feelings of others

V

vandal   one who willfully or ignorantly destroys or disfigures

W

well-mannered   having or showing good manners; polite

SUGGESTIONS FOR ADMINISTRATORS

Establish a School Behavior Code with the following components:

1. Establish school rules with input from the Student Council, the student body, staff, and administration.
2. Hold a contest to choose a school motto such as

I CAN AT _____
school name

or _____ CARES
school name

3. Acknowledge good behavior by distributing certificates

_____ WAS CAUGHT BEING GOOD
student name

AT _____
school name

or _____ IS A GOOD CITIZEN
student name

AT _____
school name

4. Determine a system of Rewards and Consequences with input from the Student Council, student body, staff, and administration.

Have occasional assemblies to remind students of the Behavior Code and to acknowledge those students who exhibit good personal and social skills.
Prepare bulletin board displays that:

1. Remind students of Behavior Code and School Motto.
2. Recognize those students exhibiting good personal and social skills.
3. Use themes to teach about:

- politeness (i.e., magic words in many languages)
- the diversity of important personages in their state: authors, athletes, inventors, educators, musicians, politicians, etc.

212

Inform community organizations about the program and i[...]

1. Write letters to groups such as the Cub Scouts, After Scho[...] gram, athletic groups, etc.
2. Write articles for the local newspaper explaining the program a[...] eliciting support from businesses in the area.

Send home all completed activities, games, and songs so that parents ar[...] the effort being made in school to improve the personal and social skills of the s[...] In addition send them the sheet "Suggestions for Parents" so they are able to [...] their children at home.

PARENTS

Date _____

...volving our students in activities to ...called *Behavior Smart* by Antonia

...vement are welcomed.

...pleted activities as they are sent home.

Listed on the next page are some suggestions you may wish to try at home to help your child.

Thank you for your anticipated cooperation.

_____
Teacher

(Overlapping page, partially visible, rotated text:)
...vite their cooperation:
...Pro-
...aware of
...udents.
...assist

SUGGESTIONS T

You can help by doing the following:

1. Make a daily habit of using and expecting your chi[...] magic words.

2. Set good examples in every social situation.

3. Avoid prejudicial statements and bring reason to any that [...] child makes.

4. Have realistic expectations for your child's behavior.

5. Prepare your child for an occasion (going to a restaurant, attending a religious service, etc.), what will happen, and how you expect him/her to behave.

6. Remove your child from a place and/or other people rather than yell, slap, etc.

7. Supervise your child's hygiene and grooming.

8. Explain to your child that having good personal and social skills will make him/her welcome and confident *anywhere*.

PARENTS

to use the

our

Inform community organizations about the program and invite their cooperation:

1. Write letters to groups such as the Cub Scouts, After School Program, athletic groups, etc.
2. Write articles for the local newspaper explaining the program and eliciting support from businesses in the area.

Send home all completed activities, games, and songs so that parents are aware of the effort being made in school to improve the personal and social skills of the students. In addition send them the sheet "Suggestions for Parents" so they are able to assist their children at home.

LETTER TO PARENTS

Date _____

Dear Parent,

In addition to our regular curriculum we are involving our students in activities to develop their personal and social skills from a book called *Behavior Smart* by Antonia Ballare and Angelique Lampros.

Your reinforcement and involvement are welcomed.

Look for completed activities as they are sent home.

Listed on the next page are some suggestions you may wish to try at home to help your child.

Thank you for your anticipated cooperation.

_____
Teacher

SUGGESTIONS TO PARENTS

You can help by doing the following:

1. Make a daily habit of using and expecting your child to use the magic words.
2. Set good examples in every social situation.
3. Avoid prejudicial statements and bring reason to any that your child makes.
4. Have realistic expectations for your child's behavior.
5. Prepare your child for an occasion (going to a restaurant, attending a religious service, etc.), what will happen, and how you expect him/her to behave.
6. Remove your child from a place and/or other people rather than yell, slap, etc.
7. Supervise your child's hygiene and grooming.
8. Explain to your child that having good personal and social skills will make him/her welcome and confident *anywhere*.